Wilfred Thesiger

was born in Addis Ababa in 1910 and educated at Eton and at Magdalen College, Oxford.

When he was twenty-three, Thesiger made his first expedition into the country of the Danakil. In 1935 he joined the Sudan Political Service and, at the outbreak of war, was seconded to the Sudan Defence Force. He later served in Abyssinia, Syria, and with the SAS in the Western Desert, and was awarded the DSO.

His journeys have won him the Founder's Medal of the Royal Geographical Society; the Lawrence of Arabia Medal; the Livingstone Medal of the Scottish Royal Geographical Society; and the Burton Memorial Medal.

His writing has won him the Heinemann Award; the Fellowship of the Royal Society of Literature; and an honorary D. Litt. from the Universities of Leicester and of Bath.

In 1968 he was made CBE. He is Honorary Fellow of the British Academy and Honorary Fellow of Magdelen College, Oxford. He was honoured with a KBE in 1995.

D0111498

WILFRED THESIGER

My Kenya Days

Flamingo

An Imprint of HarperCollins*Publishers*

Flamingo
An Imprint of HarperCollins*Publishers*
77–85 Fulham Palace Road,
Hammersmith, London W6 8JB

Published by Flamingo 1995
9 8 7 6 5 4 3

First published in Great Britain by
HarperCollins*Publishers* 1994

Author photograph by Paul Harris

ISBN 0 00 638392 0

Set in Linotron Meridian

Printed in Great Britain by
Omnia Books Limited, Glasgow

For Alexander Maitland

Contents

Acknowledgements

THIS BOOK WAS WRITTEN under considerable difficulties. Owing to the ever-increasing failure of my sight, I can no longer read or write. I have only been able to compose the book with the enthusiastic cooperation of my close friend and official biographer, Alexander Maitland, to whom I dictated it. We drafted the first chapter in London, in July 1992; Alex then brought it with him here to Maralal, where we worked on it during October and November 1992, and again at Maralal in April 1993, when the rest of the book was dictated and all of it revised. I have never dictated anything before and in consequence the style of this book differs from the previous books which I wrote down and was able to read and re-read at my leisure. I did, however, find that listening to a sentence, or even the sound of a word, read back to me helped to get it right quicker and more easily than just looking at it on a page. Almost every passage had to be read to me both in its original form and again several times to revise it. Alex showed unfailing patience when I asked him to re-read a page or more for the fifth or sixth time and often made valuable suggestions while we were doing so. It astounds me that he insists emphatically that he has really enjoyed doing this work; I found it a great help to be able to discuss its contents with him as I dictated them and I very much enjoyed working together with him.

I have written a number of books: *Arabian Sands*; *The Marsh*

Arabs; Desert, Marsh and Mountain: the World of a Nomad; a book of photographs, *Visions of a Nomad*; and an autobiography, *The Life of My Choice*. These cover all of my life until 1960 when I came to Kenya. I should have been sorry not to have written about the Kenya years; it now pleases me to have done so and compensates me for the labour involved. I have begun this book with an introductory chapter describing my life until I came to Kenya and the events which influenced it and induced me to live in Kenya as I do today. There would be no necessity for anybody who had read, for instance, *The Life of My Choice*, to read this chapter, but even for them without the background knowledge the Introduction provides, much that is in *My Kenya Days* might be incomprehensible.

Frank Steele insisted that I should write this book and now that I have done so I am grateful for his persistence. With his knowledge of Kenya, Frank has given me much valuable assistance and advice and it has been a pleasure for me to recall the journeys we did together. Lucinda McNeile, my editor at HarperCollins, has shown great skill and patience. *Visions of a Nomad*, that superb book of pictures, was Ron Clark's creation. I had taken the photographs and Ron selected those in the book from thousands of others, reproduced them, designed their layout and produced the book. Once again in *My Kenya Days* he has selected and laid out photographs taken by me. Siddiq Bhola and his family at Maralal helped Alex and me in many ways. George Webb, Mike Shaw and Melinda Maillard have all encouraged me to write this book and have assisted in its production. Here in Maralal, Rupalen Lekakwar, Laputa's younger brother, has helped me to confirm the details of Samburu customs and the spelling of Samburu names. They are too numerous to list here, but I want to thank most warmly my European friends and others of many races and tribes in

Kenya for countless acts of kindness and hospitality to me over the years in Kenya.

While writing this book, I have referred constantly to the diaries which I have kept. In most cases these amounted to little more than brief jottings, but those covering 1968–70 were more expansive. My mother always kept the letters which I wrote to her whenever I had an opportunity and they contained detailed descriptions of my journeys from 1960 until 1973 when she died. I should have found it virtually impossible to write this book had these letters not been available. I have also kept a list of my journeys, year by year, which proved a valuable framework for the book; and I am familiar with my photographs of Kenya and Tanzania, of which I have a very large number, and their recollection has assisted my memory of people and events.

When I recently visited the Pitt Rivers Museum I was impressed by their photographic section, especially by the care they took to preserve and treat scientifically the photographs and the negatives they had acquired. I felt at once that this was the place for my own collection of photographs. I have now presented my complete collection of photographs, prints and negatives, to the Pitt Rivers Museum in recognition of the four happy years I spent at Oxford. Similarly I have given all the manuscripts of my books to Eton College, which has meant so much to me.

WILFRED THESIGER,
Maralal, Kenya
April 1993

Glossary

addax	large north African antelope with twisted horns
ambach	tree with a soft, light wood used for making canes
ankus	Indian mahout's elephant goad
Barbary sheep	north African wild sheep with large horns
barbel	freshwater fish with fleshy filaments hanging from the mouth
Beisa oryx	one of five species of oryx, large antelope with long straight horns that inhabit desert or semi-desert country
boma	collection of administrative buildings and officials' dwellings; native huts enclosed by a fence
chapli	strap-on sandal
chital	Indian spotted deer
civet	very large nocturnal carnivore akin to the cat family (civet cat)
duiker	small antelope (South African Dutch *duikerbok*)
duka	a native shop
gaur	Indian wild ox
genet	species akin to the civet cat, but smaller
gerenuk	long-necked browsing antelope
Greater kudu	large antelope with long spiral horns
hagenia	tree of the family Rosaceae
klipspringer	small antelope, found in rocky surroundings (South African Dutch)
laibon	a sorcerer
lammergeier	large bearded vulture with six-foot wingspan (also spelled lammergeyer)
langur	Indian long-tailed monkey
luggah	seasonal dry watercourse

mahout	elephant driver
manyatta	Samburu or Maasai encampment, enclosed by a fence of sticks and branches
mountain nyala	a large antelope, indigenous to Ethiopia, with a resemblance to the Greater kudu
panga	a long-bladed chopper used for cutting trees and bushes
podocarpus	variety of large evergreen forest tree
sambhar	the largest Indian deer, a forest dweller (also sambar)
serval	tawny, black-spotted African tiger cat
Shifta	widely used Amharic term for bandits
shuka	large cloth hung over the often naked body from one shoulder
tankwa	papyrus canoe with a pointed prow and raised deck used on Lake Tana, Ethiopia
topi	antelope akin to the hartebeest; called 'tiang' in the Sudan

Note

The Samburu and Turkana, like other tribes, use the Roman script, but there is no one recognized system of spelling in that script and this has led to a variety of spellings of Samburu and Turkana names. For example, the river which is the southern boundary of Samburuland was spelt phonetically by the early explorers as Uaso Nyiru and this spelling often appears on maps; but later attempts to make the letters more representative of the spoken Samburu have resulted in spellings such as Ewaso Nyiro, Ewaso Ng'iro and Wuaso Ng'iro. Similarly we have Nyiru and Ng'iro for the Samburu sacred mountain west of South Horr. I have tried as far as possible to be consistent in my choice of spelling.

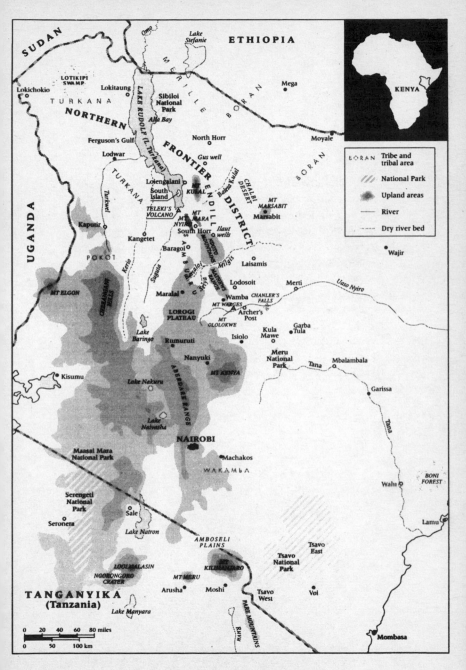

Introduction

I AM CERTAIN THAT the first nine years of my life have influenced everything that followed. I was born in Addis Ababa in 1910, the first English boy to be born in Abyssinia, as it was then called, where my father was the British Minister in charge of the Legation. Abyssinia was almost entirely dissociated from Western civilization. In 1910 the railway only went as far as Dire Dawa and from there my parents journeyed to Addis Ababa with animal transport. In 1913 my father trekked from Addis Ababa to Nairobi to discuss with the Governor various matters relating to the frontier with British East Africa, now Kenya. He then followed my mother on leave to England and, when war was declared, he obtained permission from the Foreign Office to serve in France with the Intelligence Branch until his leave expired. He had served as a captain in the army during the Boer War. He then went back to Addis Ababa, still travelling with animal transport. Of these two journeys to and from Dire Dawa, I still have faint memories and images: the sound of hyenas round campfires at night; camels and tall men with spears at waterholes.

The Emperor Menelik died in 1913. He had vastly extended his empire by overcoming and incorporating the tribes to the south, east and west. He founded his capital at Addis Ababa ('the new flower'); previously it would have been on Abyssinia's southern border. Now it was almost in the centre of his empire. Menelik's nephew Lij Yasu, a cruel, vicious boy, succeeded him, though he was never crowned. He converted virtually to Islam and was overthrown after a ferocious battle only sixty miles from the Legation where we lived. As a small boy I watched the southern army streaming past to fight in the Battle of Sagale and, after their victory, I saw the same army come past in triumph before the newly appointed Empress Zauditu, led by Ras Tafari, who later became the Emperor Haile Selassie. Many of the troops now carried rifles, otherwise they differed in no way from the armies of the past. They marched to the throb of drums and the blare of trumpets, under waving pennants and countless jostling spearheads. Few Europeans ever saw a spectacle so utterly barbaric, savage and splendid – certainly not two little boys like my brother and myself. I saw it then, tense and restless with excitement; today, at any time, I can picture it again. It gave me a craving for colour, savagery and tradition which grew over the years into an ever-deepening distaste for so-called modern progress.

In 1917, while on leave, my father took us to India, where his brother, Lord Chelmsford, was Viceroy. On the way there we stopped first at Berbera in British Somaliland, now Somalia, where Sir Geoffrey Archer was the Commissioner, and then for a few days in Aden. General Stewart, with whom we were staying, took me down with my father and brother to where we were fighting the Turks. I stood near the guns and watched our shells bursting over the Turkish lines. From Delhi we visited Jaipur where we stayed with the Maharaja and were taken on elephants to a tiger-shoot. From India, we returned to Addis Ababa for a year, before going finally to England, where my brother and I were sent to a preparatory school in Sussex. A friendly, forthcoming little boy, who had never heard of cricket or watched a football match, I was turned into a hostile reject by my contemporaries' disbelief and scorn for my stories. Very possibly, my preference in later life for Arabs and Africans was due to this early rejection by my own kind.

Throughout these four years at school I comforted myself by recalling scenes and scenery in Abyssinia. During my first year at Eton, when I was fourteen, Haile Selassie, who as Regent was still known as Ras Tafari, came on a state visit to England. My father, who had been his trusted friend, had died four years earlier. Ras Tafari invited my mother and myself to call on him. As we finally left the room, I said, 'There is one thing, sir, I want to do more than anything in the world and that is to return to your country.' And he replied with that gentle smile of his, 'One day you shall come as my guest.' Five years later I spent my long vacation from Oxford working my way as a fireman on a tramp steamer round the Mediterranean. I returned to the Milebrook, our home in Radnorshire, where two letters awaited me. One was a personal invitation from Ras Tafari, shortly to be crowned as the Emperor Haile Selassie, to his Coronation; the other was a notification from the Foreign Office that I, a boy of nineteen, was to be attached to the Duke of Gloucester's mission to the Emperor's Coronation. What man other than Haile Selassie would have thought of remembering such a promise to a fourteen-year-old boy? Mine was, indeed, the only private invitation to his Coronation. I took with me a .318 Westley Richards rifle and was determined that I should not return to England until I had done some big-game hunting. The idea of hunting big game had obsessed me since I was about six years old. As a boy my favourite reading had been Sir Percy Fitzpatrick's *Jock of the Bushveld*; and when I was only seven years old, which I can remember because of the influenza epidemic at that time, Major Powell-Cotton's *A Sporting Trip through Abyssinia* was the book that absorbed me most. When I was nine and had just gone to my prep school, John Buchan's *Prester John* took its place. It was an unexpected book to be written at the end of the last century since its hero was a black man, a Zulu leading his people against the whites. Certainly, it had a profound and lasting influence on my life. From now on my heroes were often black- or brown-skinned men: Zulus, Abyssinians, Dervishes at Omdurman and, later, Abd al Karim of the Rif in Morocco and Sultan Pasha of the Druzes, who both fought against the French.

Back in Addis Ababa, I saw views of the mountains and the surrounding country which I had often remembered so vividly at school. I saw once more the pageantry and ceremony of the past, but by now it was tarnished. There were a few cars in the streets – there had been none when I left – and the Imperial Guard was now dressed in khaki instead of carrying gilt-decorated shields and long, curved swords. And there were journalists, thrusting and pushing themselves forward to get a spectacular view or a photograph.

Ten days later, when the ceremonies were over, I went down into the country of the Danakil, the Abyssinian name for the Afar, which lies between the escarpment and the coast, but only for a short distance to hunt. At first, our Ambassador, Sir Sidney Barton, had objected to my going there with my caravan by myself, for this tribe had a murderous reputation. Among the Danakil what mattered most in a man's life was to kill and castrate as many men as possible. With practice I learned to tell at a glance from a man's decorations how many he had killed. I was down in this low, hot country on either side of the Awash River for a month, and no month in my life has had more important consequences. If we were involved in trouble, which was a distinct possibility, no one could come to our assistance and men trusted me with their lives. After this experience there could be no going back. I had seen the Awash River disappear somewhere far off in the desert ahead of us – no foreigner knew what happened to it. Already the challenge to find out was irresistible. I went back to Oxford for three years determined to solve this problem. An entire Egyptian army under Munzinger had been massacred somewhere down there sometime in the past and two Italian expeditions had also been wiped out. Two years previously Nesbitt had followed the river down as far as the boundary of Aussa, but the Sultan had refused him permission to enter this legendary land. It was rumoured that somewhere in that Sultanate, amid forests and lakes, the Awash River disappeared. For the next three years I planned to penetrate there at all costs and solve this problem.

After a nine-month expedition I had achieved my ambition. I had followed the Awash River through the length of Aussa and beyond it into the desert where it ended in a considerable sodium lake with no exit, and from there had reached the coast at Tajura. By then I had accomplished the seemingly impossible. At the time, I was twenty-four years old, with only one month's previous experience of travelling in Africa. But for the presence of Umar, my incomparable Somali headman, I would have got nowhere. And yet I was the driving force that kept the expedition going. He led and inspired the forty or more men, Christians and Muslims of different races, who constituted my followers so that there was never a dispute among them. He successfully negotiated on my behalf with murderous tribal headmen and finally with the xenophobic Sultan of Aussa himself and, despite my blunders, guarded my reputation among my men.

Back in London in 1935 I was accepted by the Sudan Political Service, a small but very select body administering the

Anglo-Egyptian condominium. The Union Jack flew side by side with the Egyptian flag over all Government buildings. Here again I was unbelievably lucky. I might have been posted to one of the towns or conventional administration centres; instead I was sent to Northern Darfur under Guy Moore. Guy Moore was the District Commissioner and I was his assistant. We were the only two Englishmen in the largest district in the Sudan, a district merging into the Libyan desert, inhabited by a variety of Muslim tribes, of Berber, Arab and Negro origin. Ours were the only two motor vehicles in the district but we travelled almost always on camels. At the end of the First World War, Guy Moore had been an administrative officer in Iraq and he spoke fluent Arabic. Six months later, when he went on leave, I found myself in sole charge of the district. I had ample opportunity to hunt dangerous game as I had long dreamed of doing. If a lion killed an animal belonging to these tribesmen, they rode it down and without shields closed in on it and speared it to death. All too frequently one or more was killed and others mauled. I often rode with them and shot the bayed lion as it charged, not infrequently at close range. Here I shot thirty lion, most of them in this manner. I have never baited for a lion or sat up for one at night, and would never have contemplated doing so.

When Guy Moore and I were together in Kutum, the village which was our headquarters, we always joined each other in the evening. He was a fascinating man to talk to and perhaps influenced me more than any other man has ever done. The two years I spent there were, I believe, the happiest of my life. At the end of two years I was to be posted to a town. I had an interview with Sir Angus Gillan, the Civil Secretary, who ran the Service, and asked him to let me resign from the permanent service and rejoin as a contract District Commissioner with the undertaking that I should only serve in the wildest and remotest areas. Though reluctant to let me, as he saw it, wreck my career, he eventually agreed, and shortly afterwards posted me to the swamps of the Western Nuer District in the southern Sudan. There I joined Wedderburn-Maxwell, the DC, on the paddle-steamer which was the district headquarters. We travelled everywhere and almost continuously through the swamps with our naked, warlike porters. The district had only been occupied and administered for sixteen years; hardly any English person other than District Officers had ever travelled there. It teemed with animals and I shot them to feed my porters, and hunted more lion as well as buffalo and elephant. On one occasion, I joined a Nuer party hunting hippo and speared and killed one myself. But though I enjoyed being with the Nuer, I craved to be back in Northern Darfur.

Just before Italy entered the Second World War, I joined the Sudan Defence Force and when she did, served under Wingate in his guerrilla warfare in Gojjam. For me this campaign was in the nature of a crusade to drive out the Italians and to restore Haile Selassie to his throne. Wingate felt the same. An extraordinary, controversial figure, he succeeded, with two battalions in a campaign of his own, in driving forty thousand Italians out of Gojjam and finally accepted the surrender of twelve thousand at the head of one weak company. No other officer, either in General Platt's army which invaded Abyssinia from the Sudan, or in General Cunningham's which entered from Kenya, could have achieved the same result. From Abyssinia I was transferred to Syria where I was second-in-command to Gerald de Gaury and helped to raise the Druze Legion to fight against the Vichy French; I met Sultan Pasha, my boyhood hero, during this campaign. I was with the Special Operations Executive in Syria for a time until, in November 1942, I was accepted into the SAS by David Stirling. Working behind the enemy lines, we reached Enfidaville in Tunisia.

When the war ended in Africa, Haile Selassie asked me to return to Ethiopia as political advisor to his eldest son, now the ruler of Wollo, one of the five northern provinces. This request I could not refuse, but the result was the most frustrating year of my life. I resigned, and two days before leaving the country chanced to meet O.B. Lean in Addis Ababa. He offered me, and I accepted, the job of investigating locust outbreak centres in the deserts of southern Arabia. This was another fortuitous and decisive happening. The Empty Quarter, the great sand desert of southern Arabia, was now within my reach. Without this backing, I could never have arrived there. I spent five years travelling with the Rashid tribe on camels. I was determined when I went there to be accepted by my companions by meeting the challenge of the desert on equal terms with them. These five years were perhaps the most important in my life. Twice, with a small and select party, I crossed the Empty Quarter. However, my travels through forbidden areas incurred the resentment of King Ibn Saud and even more the Sultan of Muscat. Finally, my return there was barred to me by the British Resident in the Gulf.

Afterwards I travelled extensively in Iraqi Kurdistan, then in 1950 went to the Marshes of southern Iraq and found there a life which appealed to me. I lived continuously with the Marshmen for seven years until 1958, except during the unbearably humid summers when I travelled extensively in the Karakorams and the Hindu Kush. I was intending to return to the Marshes in the autumn of 1958 when, in a revolution in Baghdad, the King and Royal Family were murdered and the

British Embassy was burned. I realized at once that another chapter in my life had closed.

I had grown up very conscious and proud of the British Empire, the most extensive that the world has ever seen. I myself am convinced that no empire in world history has been its equal in humanity and benign dedication to the welfare of its subjects. The years I served in the Sudan certainly confirmed this view. Today anti-colonial feeling, fostered by the Americans, has led to the Empire being criticized, even condemned, by those who believe that it dominated and exploited its subjects.

Whenever I have asked detractors of the Empire or anyone else to give me an instance of any atrocity ever committed anywhere at any time with the approval of the British administration, the answer I have invariably received has been – the incident at Amritsar in India, in 1919, when Brigadier-General Dyer ordered his troops to fire into a crowd of demonstrators. As a result, more than three hundred people were killed and a thousand or more were wounded; but this was an appalling personal misjudgement by Dyer and was in no way justified by Government policy. In contrast to France's determined but ultimately unsuccessful attempt to hold Indo-China and Algeria by force, Britain parted with her Empire gradually and without violence. There were appalling massacres on the partition of India but these were the result of inter-communal violence between Muslims and Hindus, which the few British troops left in India were unable to prevent.

Kenya's Independence Day, 12 December 1963, afforded a perfect example of Britain's attitude to the handover of power. The Duke of Edinburgh was the Queen's representative in Nairobi on that occasion. At midnight, as the Union Jack was lowered and before the Kenya flag was raised, Prince Philip apparently turned to Jomo Kenyatta, one of the most remarkable Africans of our age, and said to him: 'Are you sure you wouldn't like to change your mind?' This has always symbolized for me the friendly manner in which Britain parted with her Empire.

I remember an American author writing, 'the British left the Sudan like gentlemen'. Nothing we could have done would have prevented the chaos and conflict which rages there today. It might have been avoided had the south been divided from the north on Independence. But the Sudan was an Anglo-Egyptian condominium and Egypt would never have agreed to this. For me this violent outcome has been a personal tragedy.

Ever since my time in Northern Darfur with Guy Moore, it has been people, not places, not hunting, not even exploration, that have mattered to me most. Travelling with the Rashid in and around the Empty Quarter I had felt completely satisfied. Their society reflected a way of life which produced a nobility among them which was almost universal and a loyalty that was absolute, for which any of us would have killed. I would gladly have remained with them indefinitely, but further access was denied me. Again, but in a lesser key, among the Marsh Arabs I found a life which satisfied me, but once again access to them was eventually denied me. In Northern Darfur, then in Arabia and now in the Marshes, for the third time the life I cherished had been taken from me. I now hoped to find it elsewhere, possibly among the camel-owning tribes of northern Kenya.

CHAPTER ONE

Journey to Lake Rudolf

FOR TWO MONTHS IN 1959 I had been travelling with mule transport from Addis Ababa to the Kenya frontier. I was disappointed by the lack of game animals seen on the way to Mega, a small township some forty miles from the Kenya frontier, since wild animals had been abundant there in the accounts which I had read about this country as a boy. By now they had been virtually exterminated. I travelled through country conquered by Menelik at the end of the nineteenth century and added to the Ethiopian empire. It bore no resemblance to the five historic provinces of the north – Tigre, Begemder, Gojjam, Wollo, Amhara – with which I was familiar.

By the time I reached Mega, a journey of some four hundred miles, my shoes were worn out but the Vice-Consul in Mega, Ian Reeman, advised me to go to Moyale where he thought I would be able to get others. I did not have a permit to cross the frontier from Ethiopia into Kenya, but at Moyale the DC, George Webb, made me welcome. I told him that I must get another pair of shoes, and that evening George Webb sent for a cobbler, told him to measure my feet and to have a pair of strong *chapli* sandals ready by breakfast time. I found George Webb a quite exceptionally able linguist, a man dedicated to the work he was doing and fascinating to talk to. Ever since I was a boy I had been interested in the Northern Frontier District of Kenya (the NFD as it was more generally known).

While I was a child in Addis Ababa British officials serving on the frontiers of the Sudan, Kenya and British Somaliland came up on various occasions to see my father to discuss tribal raids and other problems they were having with the Ethiopians. While staying with us, such men as Arnold Hodson, Consul in southern Ethiopia, had told me stories of tribal raids and lion hunts and I had felt that this would be the life for me. As a boy in Ethiopia and later at school I had dreamt of exploration and of hunting big game. In the Sudan, five years before the Second World War, I took every opportunity to hunt and I shot elephant, buffalo and many lion. Now, however, I only wished to shoot an occasional animal for food. Over the years I had read a number of books about the NFD and the tribes that lived there – for instance, *The Ivory Raiders* by Major H. Rayne which my mother had given me for my fourteenth birthday. Now, talking to George Webb in the evenings, I heard a lot at first hand about tribes such as the Boran, Turkana and Rendille who lived there. He told me that a special permit was needed before anyone who was not a government official was allowed into that area, and this of course added to my determination to go there.

From Moyale I trekked back to Addis Ababa along the east side of the Rift Valley and its lakes. The next year, 1960, I made an arduous journey lasting several months from Addis Ababa, following the east side of the Blue Nile to Lake Tana; from there, I travelled through the Simien Mountains and then back to Addis Ababa by way of Lalibela and Magdala. Later the same year Frank Steele and I had planned to travel southwards from Addis Ababa to Lake Rudolf in the NFD.

I had met Frank Steele in 1951 in Iraq where he was the Vice-Consul in Basra, while I was living in the Marshes. I went into Basra occasionally to stay with him and his wife Angela to get a hot bath and a civilized meal in their house. Frank visited me in the Marshes and spent several days with me travelling about in my canoe. After the War, he had served for two years in northern Uganda where he had hunted, particularly elephant, and done some game control and conservation work. Like me, Frank enjoyed travelling simply in remote places. I had always preferred to travel on my own, but I felt that here was somebody I could happily travel with. We soon became close friends.

We had planned later that year for Frank to join me in Addis Ababa from Beirut, where he was stationed, and then to travel southwards to Lake Rudolf. However, the Ethiopians refused to give us permits on the grounds that the country was too disturbed. We therefore decided to travel to the lake through the Northern Frontier District of Kenya.

On 7 November 1960 I flew to Nairobi to meet Frank who was due to arrive a few days later. There, in the setting of the New Stanley Hotel, I felt utterly lost. I knew nobody in Nairobi and had no idea how to set about getting the necessary permit to enable Frank and myself to enter the NFD. I had, however, been given the name of someone in the administration and I went and saw him the morning after my arrival. I explained what I wanted to do and he advised me to get in touch with George Webb. I said, 'I can't go all the way up to Moyale just to see George Webb,' to which he replied, 'You needn't, he's here. He is the Number Two in Security and Defence.' I rang George immediately. He sounded surprised but pleased to hear me. 'I'll pick you up at one o'clock at the New Stanley. I've got a great barn of a house near the game park. Why not come and stay?' I was delighted and reassured to see him again. The next day he introduced me to the Governor, Sir Patrick

Renison, who gave me a special permit which authorized Frank and me to go wherever we wished in the NFD.

The NFD, bordering Uganda, Sudan, southern Ethiopia and Somalia, covered northern Kenya. The greater part was desert, inhabited by camel-owning nomad tribes. The exception was a northward extension of the plateau of the White Highlands occupied by the pastoral cattle-owning Samburu; to the west the Samburu plateau, 7000–8000 feet high, fell abruptly into the Rift Valley, and to the north and east less abruptly to the low, hot country beneath it.

After Frank and I had arrived in Nairobi we went to see Ian Grimwood, the Chief Game Warden, and he agreed to give us a game licence to shoot animals for food while we were on this safari. He suggested one animal, non-specified, a week. I said, 'Make it two, just in case in one week we need two animals; but don't worry, we shall only shoot an occasional animal for meat.'

From Nairobi, Frank and I went to Isiolo, the provincial headquarters of the NFD. In those days the government houses had attractive, well-tended gardens which have since disappeared. Today most of their owners grow maize in them. I never cared for Isiolo with its predominantly Somali inhabitants. Just beyond the town, a barrier across the road marked the entrance to the NFD. We called on Peter Walters, the Provincial Commissioner, at his house. He was in his garden, where an elephant had destroyed some of the flowers the night before. He took us into his office and we showed him our permit. I got the impression that Walters was slightly indignant that he had not been consulted before it was given to us. I told him that we planned to travel north to Lake Rudolf, then round the north side of Mount Kulal and across to Marsabit where Frank, his leave being up, would have to return to

London. From Marsabit I planned to travel south-west to Ilaut and Baragoi on my way to Lodwar. From there I would go on to Lake Baringo and then to Maralal, where I would end my journey. Frank and I were both looking forward enormously to this trip through areas visited only occasionally by an official on duty.

While we were in Isiolo, we called on George Adamson, the Game Warden, who gave us some useful advice about our journey. He and his wife Joy, and Elsa the lioness they had reared, were already well known in Kenya and after Joy had written *Born Free* were to become world-famous.

We started our journey from Kula Mawe, east of Isiolo, where we hired six camels and five men, two of whom were Somali camelmen. Kula Mawe acquired its strange name ('eat a stone') when some years previously a policeman and his young son were travelling to Garba Tula. Too late to get there that day, the policeman decided they should spend the night under a tree. They had no food with them and his son asked him what they were going to eat. The impatient father turned on him and said 'Kula mawe!' ('Eat a stone!'), a name remembered when, soon afterwards, a village was built there.

From Kula Mawe we took four days to reach Archer's Post, where a bridge crosses the Uaso Nyiro River, travelling through rolling country sometimes covered with scrub and sometimes open and grassy. We saw a lot of game: a cheetah and many oryx, eland, Grant's gazelle, impala and zebra. The zebra were very tame. Archer's Post had been established by Geoffrey Archer in 1909 as a forward post for the administration. Now it was a small village. As a boy, I had known Sir Geoffrey Archer when he was the Commissioner in British Somaliland and he had come to Addis Ababa for Zauditu's coronation as Empress in 1917. Later we had stayed with him in Berbera on our way to India, the first British children ever to have been in British Somaliland. A great giant of a man, he had been especially kind to my brother Brian and me, taking us on expeditions along the coast where we shot birds with the .410 which he lent us.

I left Frank at Archer's Post to get the camels injected against tsetse fly while I went on ahead by lorry to Wamba. At Wamba, a pleasing cluster of houses at the southern end of the Mathews Range, I stayed with the District Officer, David Bennett, who had been an instructor in an Outward Bound school in Cumberland. Together we climbed through thick forest to the top of Warges, the 9000-foot mountain immediately behind Wamba which dominated the town, and from there we had a magnificent view. In the forest were some enormous podocarpus, a tree I remembered from Ethiopia, large juniper trees, crotons, wild olives and others which I did not recognize. The podocarpus trees were covered with lichen and we saw a lot of colobus monkeys and the tracks and droppings of what we thought was a giant forest hog. We also found tracks of several herds of buffalo and masses of elephant droppings, but these were two or three days old. Next day we climbed another, rather difficult peak, and then did a twenty-mile walk northwards through the forest. There were elephant all round us in the forest and the guides saw two. We also heard a rhino. Eventually, we were picked up at the end of the forest in Bennett's Land Rover. We had to search for the Land Rover for some time before we found it and were half-expecting to have to walk all the way back to Wamba. I was glad to have seen this forest for I had not seen its like before. Frank arrived the following day from Archer's Post and the next day we set off on foot with our camels.

As on all my journeys travelling on foot with animals in

Above Landscape near Kula Mawe

Right With Frank Steele,
my companion on the journey
to Lake Rudolf

OPPOSITE
Above Turkana at Kurungu near
South Horr

Below Goat herd at South Horr

Previous page Samburu at South Horr

Above Lava desert on the
approach to Lake Rudolf –
difficult going for camels

Right Lake Rudolf:
El Molo children and
raft; (*above opposite*)
leaving the lake to circle
the northern end of
Mount Kulal

Above A Rendille hut

Opposite Rendille warriors

Below Rendille fetching water from the wells at Ilaut

Above Emaciated Turkana woman on the Kerio

Right Turkana woman with her gourd in the Suguta valley

OPPOSITE

Above left Turkana with nose ornament on the Kerio

Above right Turkana with headdress

Below Turkana having his hair dressed

Above Zebra shot by me to feed starving Pokot

Opposite Young Pokot warriors in Amaya

Overleaf Lake Baringo

Below Pokot woman and Pokot warrior at Tanglebwye

Kenya, we lived simply. We had no tables, chairs or lamps; we had a tent but seldom used it. We slept in the open in a group with our men and the camels. On one occasion, when it rained heavily, we covered our food, kit and ourselves with the cow hides from the camel harnesses. We carried water between water holes which were never more than four days from one to the next, unlike in Arabia where wells could be as much as fourteen days apart. Sometimes we drank from running streams but at other times water that was so polluted and foul as to be barely drinkable.

As our men loaded the camels at dawn we drank some coffee but ate nothing, and then moved off. At the midday halt, we drank a lot of tea but generally our only meal was in the evening and consisted of rice and stew. On one occasion when I had cooked sandgrouse, Frank maintained it was the best meal he had ever eaten; he remembers the meal to this day.

Most of the time we were in no particular hurry; and seldom did more than about seven hours a day, with a midday halt, but sometimes we kept going without a break, and occasionally we travelled at night to avoid the heat. We camped on water whenever possible; if we stopped at midday, we chose a spot where there was shade, and grazing for the camels. When we had camped, Frank and I might wander up a nearby hill for the view or go to look for elephant or try and shoot something for the pot.

All the tribes in northern Kenya, other than the cattle-owning Samburu living in the Highlands, owned large herds of camels. None of these tribes ever rode on camels; they used some of them for carrying their possessions, and sometimes women and children while they were on the move. The exception to this were the Turkana who never loaded their camels, even to fetch water. It has always seemed strange to me that

17

the Somalis have never ridden camels, in view of their association with the Arabs in southern Arabia. We walked beside our loaded camels. Nowadays tourists visiting this area can ride camels on specially organized camel safaris.

On our way to the Mathews Range, we went through hilly, stony country, some of it thickly covered with bush, and then continued northwards with the Range on our right, the mountains sometimes appearing high above us. Rather unexpectedly, we passed a big bull elephant, the first I had seen in Kenya, only fifty yards off the path. We camped for Christmas in a picturesque valley called the Ngaro Narok where there were big trees, acacias and tamarinds, and green, grassy glades, and here I saw two more elephant. That night, we heard elephant and rhino and, of course, hyenas. One rhino coming down to water almost walked into our camp in the dark and made off with a loud snort. Looking for elephant the next morning, I got within thirty yards of a black rhinoceros, the first I had ever seen, although I had previously seen a white rhino in the southern Sudan. He looked formidable as he went past, peering suspiciously in every direction.

At one camp near a luggah, some wild dogs ran along the other side and, after watching us and our camels for a while, trotted on quietly. The country appeared to be stiff with rhino. Either Frank or I went ahead to prevent our camels, tied head to tail, blundering into one of them.

We went on until we came to the Milgis, a very wide, dry watercourse which separates the Mathews Range from the Ndoto Mountains. We then made our way up a track which took us along the top of the Ndotos. After working our way along the mountain for three days we descended by Ndigiri Alauri, the 'Pass of the Camels' to the hot, scrub-covered country below.

Looking northwards from the pass, I had realized that there was nothing ahead of us but desert country to the Ethiopian frontier and far beyond. This gave me the satisfaction of knowing that all the farms, ranches and towns were far behind and that ahead of us were only scattered wells, the encampments of nomads, and wild animals. Above all, it was the wild animals which made travelling in this country so much more interesting than in southern Ethiopia, which it otherwise resembled. Here, at any time, you half-expected to walk into an elephant or a rhino. At the foot of the Pass, within a yard of where I slept, there had been a great pile of elephant droppings. The mountains covered with forest and giant euphorbia gave a background to the scene, but I craved to get back to this desert country. I could picture it to the north with its space, solitude and silence.

We seemed to have collected a good lot of men, the two Somali camelmen, an elderly Galla from the Boran tribe and two Turkana boys, one of whom, a powerfully-built lad called Ekwar, did the cooking. He remained with me for several years. We had been feeding well, with one good meal a day, and when we were near their encampments the Samburu usually gave us a goat.

I had been trying to learn Swahili so that I could manage when Frank had to leave me at Marsabit. I am not a natural linguist, although after eleven years living on my own with Arabs in southern Arabia and the Marshes of Iraq I had become fluent in that language. Struggling to learn Latin at Eton destroyed for ever any enthusiasm I might have had for conscientiously learning languages.

In the far distance to the west were the mountains on either side of South Horr for which we were heading. When we got there, South Horr was particularly attractive. It lay in the valley between Nyiru, nearly 10,000 foot high, to the west and the jagged peaks of Ol Doinyo Mara, 7000 foot high, to the east. We camped in a beautiful grove of tall, slender acacias with a clear stream of running water nearby. Today there is a large village there with some shops and cultivation; then there was nothing other than a small Somali *duka* tucked away; there we replenished our *posho* and sugar. Frank climbed Ol Doinyo Mara, but I did not accompany him because I had strained an Achilles tendon. He came back tired and thirsty, saying that the mountain seemed to consist entirely of rocks and thorn bushes and that the going had been hard and hot. But from the top, he had had a magnificent view of the desert country to the north and north-east, shimmering in the heat, and his description of this whetted my appetite for the days to come.

While Frank had been away, in the nearby forest two hundred yards from our camp, I came across a bull elephant with tusks which must have weighed 100 lb each. I got up to within twenty yards of him while he was dozing and had a good look at him, then withdrew.

After South Horr, we travelled for three hours up the valley until we came to Kurungu, a dry watercourse with a pool of water. Here we encountered four young Turkana who came into our camp, and I was surprised to see how graceful and handsome these young men were. I had not expected to find such classical features among the Turkana and, indeed, I learned later that few Turkana were as good-looking. I looked forward to seeing more of the Turkana on my return journey from Marsabit. We had been travelling through Samburu country so far; the Samburu were a tall, strikingly handsome people, I hoped that I had got some good photographs of them.

Beyond South Horr, we had a long, tiring trek. Luckily, my foot stood up well to this. Frank had made enquiries about tracks and distances to the lake and had got a frustrating variety of answers. In fact, it took us three more days. On the last two, it was hard-going, for the surrounding country was one vast lava field of boulders, red or black in colour, and we had to push on for there was no water anywhere except for what we carried. Conscious that we were approaching the lake, we expected to see it as we topped each new rise, but never seemed to do so.

Suddenly, it was there below us. Few other sights have made a greater impact on me. I saw the lake spread out beneath me, stretching towards the Ethiopian frontier where it ended 150 miles away. We had come a long way from Kula Mawe on foot and now felt a sense of achievement. I found it easy to imagine what this sight must have meant to Teleki and Von Höhnel in 1888, as they stood, surrounded by their valiant but exhausted porters, having at last reached this hitherto unknown lake after their long and perilous journey from the coast. The next day, we had a hard, seven-hour march in intense heat which eventually got us to Loiengalani. Here was an oasis with trees and some doum palms along a stream, the only fresh water I believed to be found on the shore of Lake Rudolf. Loiengalani was a surprisingly beautiful place, very peaceful, and with shimmering lights over the lake and South Island in the middle. In those days there was nothing else there, except a police post and small huts used by the District Commissioner at Marsabit and other officials on their rare visits to the lake. Now Loiengalani has developed into a town, with a mission station, a church and a lodge with extensive accommodation for tourists; shops, houses, and a conglomeration of tribal huts with an airstrip nearby. Remembering Loiengalani as I first saw it, I always resent this imposition on the lake's previously unblemished surroundings.

Peter Browning, the DC from Marsabit, happened to be there for a couple of days, which was useful as I was able to arrange with him to get me new camels at Marsabit to take me on the second half of the journey. George Adamson, the Game Warden, had arrived the previous day. He was looking for somewhere new to turn Elsa loose. Until then the Adamsons had planned to release Elsa on the edge of Meru National Park. However, the Meru had threatened to kill her if they did so. Now the Adamsons planned to turn Elsa loose up here. I liked and respected Adamson very much, and regretted that I saw so little of him, but I found his wife impossible when I met her in Isiolo. She had burst into the room while we were talking to Adamson, shouting, 'George, George! Vy have you not done vat I told you? Go down to the town and get the things I told you to get!' He tried to calm her by saying, 'Can't you see that I've got guests?' But she continued to shout, 'I don't care about your guests. Get in the car!' Thinking it over afterwards, I wondered why he had not taken her out into the bush and shot her.

Our destination after Loiengalani was Marsabit, the isolated mountain about ninety miles east of Loiengalani across the Chalbi Desert. But lying in between was Mount Kulal, an extraordinary volcanic mountain which runs north–south, parallel to and about fifteen miles east of the lake. When we said goodbye to George Adamson at Loiengalani, he had described the country to the north of Kulal with typical understatement as 'quite stony'. Our first camp after Loiengalani was a beautiful little valley with springs, doum palms and acacia trees called Lare Debach – an astonishing sight in that lava desert and looking much as Von Höhnel described it when he and Teleki camped there some seventy years earlier. We then circled the northern end of Kulal for two hard days across a desert of lava boulders. We had the greatest difficulty in getting the camels through these, often coming to a standstill while we searched for a way forward. It was intensely hot, with a tearing wind which dried us out instead of cooling us. The views were magnificent. We had a final glimpse of the lake which, Frank observed, seemed as reluctant to disappear as it had been to reveal itself. As we wanted to have a closer look at Kulal, we travelled south down its east side. A civet cat jumped out from a bush close to the path; it was the first I had ever seen and I watched with interest as it ran off up a hill. We camped in a steep-sided gorge running into Kulal with clean, fresh water holes under big spreading trees, and fresh rhino middens nearby. To rest the camels, we camped here for two nights, building big fires to keep away any rhino. Donaldson Smith, the American who led an expedition to Lake Rudolf in 1894–95, described the northern circuit of Kulal as four days of torment, marching through a fiery furnace with the sun's rays beating down with relentless fury. Even the redoubtable Lord Delamere on his expedition to the lake in 1896–98 was so disheartened and tired by the experience that instead of continuing north up the lake to Lake Stefanie, as he had intended, turned back south.

Still moving south down the side of Kulal, we camped near the entrance to El Kajarta, the great gorge that appears to split Kulal in two. Frank and I walked for about three hours into the gorge which must be one of the most extraordinary physical features in Kenya, and one of the least visited because of its remoteness. The vertical walls rose up for a thousand feet or so, sometimes overhanging and reducing the gap between them at the top to less than forty yards. We stopped at a point where the gorge narrowed sharply and here boulders made the going unpleasantly difficult. There was a pool of good water so we made some tea and then returned down the gorge to our camp.

From there we had another interesting six days, travelling fairly leisurely the eighty miles or so to Marsabit, across the Chalbi Desert where we saw many Grant's gazelle and some oryx. We were now among the Rendille, a nomadic camel-owning people, and we encountered numbers of them with their animals at various water holes. Throughout the last day we saw Marsabit ahead of us, a cloud-capped mountain, 5600 feet high, rising from the empty desert. This whole country was suffering from a severe drought and everywhere the grazing was almost non-existent. But the mountain itself was covered with forests, and I remembered that my father had gone there in 1913 on his trek to Nairobi from Addis Ababa. I still have a letter he had written to me in pencil from Laisamis, with his drawings of elephant and buffalo.

CHAPTER TWO

Marsabit to Maralal

AT MARSABIT, FRANK LEFT ME almost as soon as we arrived and I was sad for I had found him an excellent companion, very equitable and full of pleasure in everything he saw. Peter Browning had asked us to stay when we met him at Loiengalani, and I now looked forward to a week's comfort and rest in his house, and the chance of seeing the wildlife in the forest where there were some of the biggest elephant left in Africa.

Browning was friendly and hospitable and it was pleasant to rest and be comfortable for a few days. This was a wonderful place. The mountain rose from the surrounding desert, much of it under a forest of very big trees. Every morning I woke up to find the mountain covered by a thick mist which cleared away by about midday, after which it became sunny, warm and lovely. The air was crisp and cold, everything was green and sparkling, and yet only a few miles away was the real desert.

There were several craters in the forest and on one occasion, standing on the edge of the largest, Lake Paradise, Browning and I had a spectacular view of a herd of elephant immediately below us. On the way back to the house we saw Mohammed, the famous elephant whose long, pointed tusks weighed well over 100 lb a side. He was succeeded by Ahmed, an elephant with even bigger and heavier tusks; if I remember correctly, Ahmed was declared a national monument by Jomo Kenyatta.

The forest surrounded Browning's garden, and elephant and buffalo came very close to the house at night.

While at Marsabit I finished reading *A Thing to Love* by Elspeth Huxley, about the Mau Mau. It was good, but nothing like so stark and horrifying as Ruark's *Something of Value*.

From here I sent back my Boran camels to Kula Mawe with the Boran, a delightful old man whom I was sorry to lose. We had been lucky with our men, especially Ekwar, the Turkana cook-boy, and the two Somalis. From Marsabit, I kept the two Somali camelmen, Ekwar, whom I liked, and Soiyah, a well-meaning Turkana who had occasionally infuriated Frank and me by his oafishness. I took on Rendille camels and two Rendille camelmen for the rest of my journey to Lodwar, Lake Baringo and Maralal.

We made our way down from the cool, beautifully wooded mountain back to the desert. We crossed from there to Ilaut. The wells at Ilaut are deep and, I believe, never go dry: for this reason, they are of great importance, particularly to the Rendille, in times of drought.

At Ilaut we found a small shop kept by a friendly young Somali whose father had recently been killed. He was very hospitable and fed me on good food during the two days I spent there to rest the camels and myself. The wells here were close to a tree under which we camped and at night elephant came down to them to drink. Three passed within thirty yards of our camp; noiseless grey shapes in the moonlight. Zebra, too, went past, their hooves noisy on the rocks. High above our camp were the spectacular sheer-sided peaks of the Ndotos. From Ilaut, I travelled round the northern end of the Ndotos towards Baringo, through bush country which was full of rhino tracks, but we saw none. We travelled slowly, for now at last there had been rain and pools of water lay around, more than welcome after years of drought. We encountered more of the Rendille, a tribe I had immediately liked and assumed to be akin to the Somali, but who dressed like the Samburu. They were gathered here in large numbers with their camels and goats. Unlike the Samburu who own large herds of cattle, the Rendille are a camel-owning people and I enjoyed once more seeing herds of camels which for years have been my favourite animal. On more than one occasion when I was travelling in the Empty Quarter of Arabia our lives had depended on our camels' endurance. Had they collapsed we should have died. The Rashid speak of them as *ata Allah* (God's gift). My companions had an intense affection for their camels and would always undergo hardship themselves to spare them if possible. Living with the Rashid as one of them, I had learned to some extent to share their feelings.

The Rendille lived in easily moved mat shelters, similar to those I had seen when travelling in 1933–34 among the Danakil. I found the Rendille friendly and welcoming. At each encampment they gave me a sheep or a goat.

The moon was full and at one of these Rendille encampments they had a dance which started near midnight. It was spectacularly effective, with camels couched all round and the dancers' spears stuck upright in the ground. The songs were rousing and the dancing very energetic in short bursts, men and women together.

Some of them were suffering from ophthalmia and came to me for treatment. On my Danakil journey I had taken such medicines with me as had been recommended for treating any of my followers who fell sick with malaria or some other ailment, or perhaps any Danakil who asked for medicine, and thereby earn their gratitude. In Darfur I always took disinfectants, aspirin, morphine and anti-malarial medicine with me on trek. When I was in Kutum I attended our clinic to learn what I could from our Sudanese dresser.

During the seven years I spent in the Marshes where no doctor had ever been, I was often overwhelmed by the number of my patients, perhaps as many as seventy in a day. The Iraqi authorities approved of what I was doing despite the fact that I had no medical qualifications; but they did warn me that if anyone died as a result of my treatment I might have to face a criminal charge. I treated many people who were dying but no official ever said that I had been responsible for someone's death.

When I first travelled in Kenya with camels and later with a Land Rover, there were hardly any clinics in the areas which I visited. Many people would come to me asking for treatment. The doctor then in charge of the Maralal hospital, supplied me with medicines and gave me much useful advice. In recent years, a large number of Catholic churches and others of various Protestant denominations have been built throughout the tribal areas of northern Kenya. I do feel exasperated by this incessant building of churches instead of clinics. Today in Maralal, there is only a government hospital – which at present is short of drugs – and a small clinic administered by a Catholic nursing sister, but there are now some fifteen churches belonging to various denominations in and around this small town.

We were now on the edge of the Turkana country. At Baragoi, it had rained recently and the country was very green, as it had been all the way across from Marsabit. From here I planned to cross the Suguta valley and go to Kangetet, then down the Kerio river to Rudolf, and from there to follow the Turkwel river from its mouth to Lodwar. The 1960 drought had been especially severe among the Turkana, but by going this way we should not be short of water. By now I was talking some Swahili, what is known as 'up-country Swahili', an easily learned variant of the language. The men I had with me were excellent, cooperative and friendly among themselves; and I had already got rid of the only one I had disliked.

I was fascinated to see the Turkana, a numerous, virile tribe with a warlike reputation. Many of the men and boys were naked. When I reached the Kerio, I woke up one morning to find six elders waiting under a nearby tree. They were sitting on their wooden headstools which they use as pillows when they sleep. The only clothing they had between them were two European felt hats. As a result of the drought many of the Turkana were nearly starving but, moving about in small family groups, they kept their goats alive by cutting off branches from trees. They themselves survived largely by eating the husks of doum nuts, berries and other wild fruits, and by trapping and killing wild animals. On one occasion, we came across a young wart hog which had been snared and was half-hanging in the air. We ate it.

In recent years much of this forest has been cleared, especially along the Turkwel, and the Turkana have concentrated round the churches, clinics and schools established by missionaries and overseas organizations. Consequently they have forfeited their mobility, which in the past had enabled them to survive under the conditions I had witnessed in 1960. Now, most of the Turkana are increasingly dependent on outside aid and, as a result of the drought in 1992, are in a desperate way.

Heavy rain was expected any day and the clouds were indeed already banking up, but if the rains failed again this year conditions would be even worse. The 1960 drought had not, however, affected my journey, and would not, for I was following the big river beds where there was water in wells every few miles and we were carrying food for ourselves. From Baragoi to Lodwar we only once had to carry water for the night. Beyond Baragoi I travelled west to Kangetet across the Suguta, where brackish water was flowing two feet deep and fifty yards across; and then I went down the Kerio to within a few miles of Lake Rudolf, and from there across to the nearby mouth of the Turkwel and followed it up to Lodwar. The Kerio was a big riverbed fringed with bush, large acacias and doum palms on both banks. Near Kangetet, there was a strange and extensive forest of dead trees, many of them large, and I was surprised to find here the fresh tracks of elephant, one of them with a small calf, and several single ones. Otherwise I had seen almost nothing in the way of wildlife, a few Grant's gazelle and that was all. By contrast, on my journey to Marsabit with Frank Steele, we had encountered elephant, rhino, lion and hyenas, many small herds of Grant's gazelle and some oryx. The Turkana kill wild animals for food, whereas the Samburu do not and unlike the other tribes in the NFD the Turkana will eat donkeys and drink their milk. However, I was told there were elephant and buffalo along the Turkwel above Lodwar.

My family had played an important role in ensuring that the Turkana country did not become part of Abyssinia (as it was then known). In the struggle for power in Africa at the turn of the century, the Abyssinians made determined and persistent attempts to take control of the Turkana and the adjacent region of Karamoja. In early 1911, when I was one year old, my father confronted the Abyssinian government and pointed out to them that their provisional southern boundary, marked by a red line on the map attached to the 1907 Agreement between Abyssinia and the British government, ran north of the Turkana and Karamoja.

The Abyssinian government replied that no one knew where the line on the map was on the ground, that Abyssinia was in practice in occupation of this area and that the British had never occupied it. This statement was correct: the Uganda government (who were at the time nominally responsible for the Turkana and Karamoja) did not have, and the government in London would not provide, the money and resources to occupy the area. My father then wrote to the Governor of Uganda describing this meeting with the Abyssinian government; and he warned Uganda that unless they effectively occupied the Turkana and Karamoja country up to the red line, these areas would be lost to Abyssinia. By now, Uganda had the money, from exports of recently introduced cotton, to allocate resources to these areas; and late in 1911 they started to do so, eventually driving out the Abyssinians.

In support of this, another member of my family, Colonel G. Thesiger, who was then Inspector General of the King's African Rifles, made a tour of inspection of the northern area and in 1913 recommended strong military action to push the Abyssinians back over their side of the frontier.

At Lodwar, I spent an enjoyable few days with the DC, Geoffrey Hill. In this vast arid region, Lodwar had been an important administrative centre ever since the Turkana had been taken over and administered by the British. From 1906 onwards Lodwar had been the base from which frequent Ethiopian raids had been countered by Major Rayne and others. I was familiar with this area from Rayne's book, *The Ivory Raiders*, published in 1923. Lodwar was a surprisingly small town; a few European-style houses on a small hill overlooked the dry bed of the Turkwel. Behind them was a Turkana village. In those days the forest bordering the Turkwel upstream of Lodwar reached almost to the town. Jomo

Kenyatta, who after independence was to become the first president of Kenya, was in detention at Lodwar when I arrived there, but he was to be moved later to Maralal. An impressive-looking man, I saw him on a number of occasions when he reported each morning to the DC's office. I stayed on at Lodwar for two more days to get my camels injected against fly and give them time to get over the inoculation.

The last part of my trip was particularly interesting. From Lodwar, as far south as Kaputir, we travelled up the Turkwel, a large riverbed, dry at this time of year and with dense forests along both banks. One day we were marching up the riverbed when we encountered a large bull elephant and two smaller ones. They looked threatening, so we turned back, and we had to go some distance before we found a way through the forest to get round them. As there were plenty of wells in the Turkwel we were never short of water. Many naked, wild-looking Turkana were on these wells. There were evidently many buffalo in the forests along the river banks, some of which the Turkana caught with snares and drag-logs. One morning, I and a party of a dozen Turkana followed the tracks of a buffalo, with a log caught on one of its feet, through really horrid, thick bush. I was amazed that the buffalo was strong enough to prevent the log from getting entangled and bringing it to a halt. Eventually the log came loose and, as a result, we did not catch up with the buffalo.

We usually started off each morning by moonlight, an hour or so before dawn. I now went on ahead of the camels to make sure they did not walk into buffalo or elephant. One morning, we found six buffalo in the middle of the riverbed and had to shout at them to get them to move. From Kaputir, I crossed the intervening country to the Kerio at Kalosia and went up the Kerio to the foot of the Cherangani Hills, an 11,000-foot

range, and then followed the edge of the escarpment southwards. This was the country of the Pokot, or the Suk as they
were then called. To me they resembled the Turkana in appear-
ance except that they were circumcised whereas the Turkana
were not. It is curious how often tribes have been known for
years by the wrong name. For instance, it is only recently that
the Suk have been accorded their proper name, the Pokot, by
Europeans. The Danakil, as they were previously called, are
now correctly called the Afar; and the Toubou of Tibesti are
now known as the Tedda.

Eventually I reached the north end of Lake Baringo. We had
a long and rather tiring march to the lake across a dry, dusty
expanse of wait-a-bit thorn scrub through which we had,
occasionally, to cut our way, but it was well worth it when
we got there. Ahead of us were large, green trees and beyond
them a white beach of pebbles and a very blue lake. We could
see small, wooded islands and creeks, and in the distance high
mountains on the eastern and western sides of the lake. There
were some hippo in the lake near our camp and I enjoyed
watching them and hearing them grunt. I also saw occasional
crocodiles, and a pair of fish eagles that screamed as they sat
in the trees. The colours of the lake kept changing every
minute for there was a lot of cloud about. Some men and boys
belonging to the Tugen tribe brought us in plenty of fish called
tilapia, resembling perch and weighing about a pound, which
were excellent eating. They fished for them in small *ambach*
canoes made like the *tankwa* on Lake Tana. Some carried bows
with poisoned arrows. We stayed at Baringo for two days. We
were still among the Pokot until we reached the edge of the
escarpment on which Maralal lies. We had seen zebra and
impala on our way.

Maralal was an attractive station, the headquarters of the

Samburu district, situated on the plateau at about 7000 feet. The hills going up behind the station and elsewhere were partly covered with forests of wild olives and juniper, while acacia woodlands covered much of the lower ground. Maralal is only eighty miles north of the Equator and consequently it has no summer and winter. Instead, the long rains lasting from March into June and the short rains falling in October and November are separated by the dry seasons. Being virtually on the Equator, the temperature in the NFD is governed by the altitude and varies little throughout the year. I arrived in Maralal for Easter. While I was unloading my camels among some trees outside Maralal, a Land Rover drew up nearby and a military-looking man got out and said abruptly, 'Are you Wilfred Thesiger?' I said, yes; and he went on, 'I am Rodney Elliott, the Game Warden. I understand you were given permission in Nairobi to shoot two animals a week in this division. Of course, had I known about this, you most certainly wouldn't have got permission to do so. Get in the car at once and come up to the office. I want you to fill in a form saying exactly what you have shot.' Exasperated, I replied I was prepared to do so, either on foot or in his car, but only after I had got my animals unloaded and my camp pitched. He waited for me, drove me to his office and thrust a paper at me, saying, 'Fill in exactly what you have shot – where, when, and what sex.' To annoy him, I said that four months at two animals a week entitled me . . . He interrupted me, 'I'm not interested in what you are entitled to, I want to know *exactly what you did in fact shoot*.' I sat down at a desk, pulled out my notebook, fiddled about with this for some time, filled in the form and gave it to him. On it was written: two Grant's gazelle, one Thomson's gazelle and one Burchell's zebra. He looked at it, looked up in surprise and said, 'Are you sure this is all you shot?' I said, 'Yes, I had no intention of massacring your animals. I shot these gazelle for food and the zebra for some starving Pokot.' He continued to look surprised, then smiled and said, 'Well, I think you'd be more comfortable in my house than in your tent.' We have been the best of friends ever since and I have always thought of Rodney Elliott as the outstanding Game Warden in Kenya, whom it has been a privilege to know.

The following morning, Rodney Elliott took me out to show me rhinoceros. We found one almost at once and got up very close to it in thick bush. Today, all this bush has been cleared and this spot is now on the outskirts of the town. With a snort, the rhino exploded out from under our feet and I had a good, though fleeting sight of it.

Ever since I first saw one I have been fascinated by rhino, these prehistoric-looking beasts. When I arrived in Kenya in 1960 there were about 20,000 rhino in the country. Today there are at most a few hundred rhino left here. This massive destruction is of recent origin. Though rhino horn has always been valued as an aphrodisiac in Asia, and consequently some rhino were poached for this, the massive killing in more recent years was to provide rhino-horn handles for Yemeni daggers. In 1966–67 when I was in the Yemen during the Civil War I never noticed a rhino-horn handle on anybody's dagger. When I returned to the Yemen in 1977 our ambassador mentioned to me that expatriate Yemenis working in Saudi Arabia, the Gulf States and Oman were remitting back to the Yemen as much as half a million pounds a day. At that time, there was very little in the Yemen on which to spend these huge sums of money; but when the fashion for rhino-horn daggers suddenly caught on, enormous sums were available to buy the horn. This demand for rhino horn has virtually exterminated rhino not only in Kenya but throughout Africa, to me a horrifying example on a vast scale of utterly pointless human extravagance inspired by vanity.

Later in the morning, we found thirty elephant, six of them babies, in a dry riverbed about a mile from Maralal. We stayed for a long time watching them from nearby. Then in the evening we went out again and got close to a buffalo and her calf. In all, it was an unforgettable day, especially as I was with Rodney Elliott.

The *boma*, or administrative centre, with the government offices and houses of British officials, was (and still is) about half a mile from the town. It was here that Rodney Elliott lived and had his office. Maralal itself consisted of a rectangle of wide streets planted with trees and small adjoining wooden shops painted in various bright colours. In those days all the Samburu warriors, or *moran* as they were called, wore a length of red cloth knotted over one shoulder, their faces and chests often coloured with red ochre, their plaited hair long down their backs. The elders wore red blankets. All the women were draped with blue cloth. It was a peaceful and attractive place. You could spend a whole day in the town without seeing or hearing a car, though a Pakistani called Siddiq Bhola owned a garage. When I left next day for Nairobi, Siddiq took me in his car and absolutely refused to accept any payment for doing so. For thirty years, he has shown me unfailing kindness and hospitality and is now one of my closest friends.

CHAPTER THREE

Lion Country

THREE DAYS AFTER MY ARRIVAL in Nairobi from Maralal, I
went to stay with John Newbould who was working as a Pasture Research Officer at Ngorongoro, a reserve adjoining the
Serengeti National Park. Five years earlier, when he was on
an Oxford University expedition in Morocco, we had travelled
together on foot in the High Atlas and climbed to the summit
of the Toubkal massif. Since then he had suggested that when
I went back to Kenya I should come and stay with him at
Ngorongoro, which I now proceeded to do. It was now the
middle of April. John was living in a three-roomed shack on
the very edge of the Ngorongoro crater. This enormous crater
was 2000 feet deep and almost ten miles across. Further along
the crater rim the only road led down to the floor of the crater.
At that time few people visited Ngorongoro and, looking down
into it from John's house, if we saw a car we could be almost
certain that it belonged to the Warden. Sometimes John
motored me down there, at other times we went down on foot
and wandered about among the animals which we enjoyed far
more than being in a car. But there is no denying that in a car
one can get infinitely closer to lion, for instance, which will
continue to lie undisturbed within a few feet of the vehicle
itself. But I have always felt this to be unnatural.

On the green, grassy floor of the crater there was a salt lake,
numerous pans of fresh water, a stream fringed with reed beds
and a patch of forest, the whole scene rimmed by the steep

walls of the crater. This restricted area was covered with animals: herds of wildebeest, heraldic-looking creatures that grunted and frisked about, mixed with zebra and gazelle; and frequently we saw buffalo, rhino and, above all, lion, including the first black-maned lion I had ever seen. Maasai still lived here with their cattle, and I felt that they belonged here and were a traditional part of the scene, which would be diminished if they were turned out. The Maasai do not hunt and kill animals for food, though spearing lion is a challenge and is accepted as a test of courage. John and I visited one of their *manyattas* to hire donkeys for a journey in the neighbourhood. There were many *moran* here who were on good terms with John and consequently friendly.

I had often heard that the Maasai were remarkably beautiful and many of them certainly were. The warriors wore a single piece of cloth, dyed a soft, reddish brown, which fell from one shoulder over their graceful, naked bodies. All of them carried heavy, long-bladed spears and some had buffalo-hide shields decorated with coloured heraldic designs. At dawn the following day, we watched two boys being circumcised, just outside the huts in which they lived. The initiation ceremonies among the Maasai and the Samburu are similar except that the Maasai circumcise boys individually in the encampment where they live, whereas among the Samburu each clan assembles the initiates and their families in specially-built circumcision camps known as *lororas*, where they live throughout the ceremonies involved and which are burnt when they are over. Not a muscle twitched on either of the boys' faces during the long and painful operation, which is performed in a curious, complicated manner by both the Maasai and the Samburu.

During the time I was at Ngorongoro, I spent two interesting days camped in the crater with the Game Warden. As he walked back the last evening by the way we had come, he saw a black leopard. I would have given much to have seen it myself, for I have never seen one. Before I left, John and I travelled for a month with donkeys in the country surrounding the crater. Both the long and short rains had failed and the country was now drought-stricken; in consequence, we did not see as many animals as I had hoped. This year it seemed inevitable that the Maasai would lose most of their cattle.

There were several smaller craters in the area where there was a certain amount of forest. I was exploring one of these forests, following a game path with Ibach, a powerfully-built young Turkana who had joined me in Maralal, when suddenly we found ourselves in extensive beds of tall, extremely painful nettles. To give Ibach's bare legs some protection I lent him my sweater which he put on like a pair of trousers, looking very odd in consequence. I was glad to have taken on Ibach at Maralal, since he proved indefatigable and was always cheerful.

When I left Ngorongoro, John took me in his car all the way to a hotel on the Kenya coast, where I joined the Webbs who were on holiday there. It was the only hotel in the area and, except for an occasional fisherman in his outrigger canoe, we could walk indefinitely along the white sandy beach under coconut palms, rarely meeting anyone. George was anxious for me to see Lamu, feeling sure that Lamu would appeal to me, so he and I flew down there for a few days from Mombasa. Lamu was a small town of Arab origin on an island separated from the mainland by a creek. The whole of this coast had originally been occupied by Arabs from Oman. It pleased me to be back once more in this Muslim atmosphere. I enjoyed seeing the town with its narrow streets separating the tall, whitewashed houses with their elaborately carved doors, and

I was interested to meet the people here. We stayed in a dilapidated hotel called Petley's, the only one on the island. I remember once looking down through a hole in my bedroom floor and seeing people drinking at a bar in the room below. There were few Europeans in the town and mercifully there was not a single car.

I returned to Kenya in February 1962. George Webb and I had already planned to climb Kilimanjaro and we set off two days after my arrival, motoring to Moshi in Tanganyika. We spent the first night in the Kibo Hotel at the foot of the mountain, on the south side, about twenty miles from the lowest hut which was just a bare shed with bunks. We had six porters with us and a guide from the Chagga tribe, a Bantu people who live on the southern slopes of the mountain. I liked them – a cheerful people, very eager to help. We went slowly to begin with, to get ourselves acclimatized. When we got to the next hut, we met an RAF mountain-rescue expedition from Cyprus that had got into trouble. They had climbed the mountain too fast and camped in the crater at 18,500 feet. Two of them (there were eight in all) had collapsed during the night and become unconscious. The others, with their Chagga porters, had difficulty in getting them down from the crater. The two sick men were paralysed from the waist down and it looked to me as if one of them had pneumonia. It was rather a daunting start for us to meet these experts driven down off the mountain like this.

Kilimanjaro has two peaks: Kibo, a huge crater, a great dome of ice and snow 19,340 foot high; and Mawenzi, a deeply eroded, steep, jagged mountain 16,900 foot high. At 15,000 feet, they are separated by a bare stony plain, the saddle of Kilimanjaro. Here, we spent the last night in the hut at the foot of Kibo. It was bitterly cold, with snow lying about in patches on the mountainside. There had been more snow on the mountain this year than for years. The hut was cold and draughty. We spent a wretched night there and neither of us slept a wink owing to the altitude. The guide called us at 1 a.m. We had some tea and biscuits and then started off up the mountain in the dark, following his hurricane lamp. There was ashy scree at first, and then, after about 3000 feet, the slope became very steep and covered with frozen snow into which we kicked steps. This was better than it might have been, for without snow it would have been loose scree which slips back as you climb it. We toiled up this for four hours, going slowly to save ourselves and stopping every now and then for a rest, but it was too cold to stop long.

We reached the crater rim at Gilman's Point, 19,000 foot high, just as the sun rose, an orange ball seen through the blanket of cloud on the horizon, above which towered the black, jagged outline of Mawenzi. A minute or two later and the sun was clear of the cloud and flooding the slope on which we sat. Behind us was a great wall of green ice. Both of us were feeling perfectly all right, no headaches or sickness. Round the rim of the crater, the summit looked only twenty minutes away. In fact it took us two very hard hours to get there through soft snow. The last 500 feet were a desperate effort. We would go a few yards and sink down again to rest. Here we saw five wild dogs. They followed us about a hundred yards away, keeping parallel with us along the glacier on our left. It was an amazing thing to have found wild dogs at 19,000 feet, about 10,000 feet higher than they normally ever go. They looked like wolves in the snow as they followed us, or sat and watched us. I have often wondered if there is any record of mammals having been found at a higher altitude.

From the summit we had a wonderful view down into the crater: black rock, great walls of green ice and white snow. The country below us was hidden in mist and cloud so that we were above it in a world of our own. Nearby, Mawenzi rose up out of the cloud. We had a sense of achievement when we reached the summit cairn marking Kaiser Wilhelm Spitz. The wild dogs were still watching us and their tracks were then quite close to the cairn. I wondered whether they had come up in the dark or spent the night on the summit. Going down, the snow had softened in the sun so that we could descend fast, but even so it was hard work. I was glad we had come up in the dark. It would have been daunting if we could have seen the interminable slope above us. In 1953 I travelled in Hunza where I had probably been as high as the summit of Kilimanjaro when I reached the Babaghundi Pass. We were back in the hut nine hours after leaving it. Here we rested for a bit and I noticed a lammergeier circling above us. Whereas lammergeiers are frequently seen in Ethiopia, where I once saw six, circling together over a rubbish tip in Dessie, they are rare in Kenya and Tanzania. I have only seen them there three times – once on this occasion, another time on Mount Kenya and again at Hell's Gate near Naivasha where a pair nested in the cliffs until someone took their eggs. In the Samburu district, vultures and kites are equally uncommon and in all the years I have been there I have hardly ever seen one. In 1976, when perhaps two hundred cattle were slaughtered on a hillside during a Samburu initiation ceremony, only two vultures turned up and sat in one of the trees. Elsewhere, for instance, in the Maasai Mara, scores of vultures will cluster on any dead animal.

We then went down ten miles to the next hut, where we were back in the giant heath and giant groundsel country. The giant groundsel is an extraordinary plant with leaves like a cabbage on the top of a thick bare stem eight feet high made of old dead leaves. The following day we walked the twenty miles down through the forest to the hotel and from there we motored back to Nairobi. I could not have had a better companion than George Webb on this expedition.

After staying with George for a few days in Nairobi, I went up to Isiolo where I hired camels for another journey in the NFD. Lokuyie, a Samburu *moran*, had joined me for this journey. He was an impressively handsome figure with his distinctively-plaited hair, his red *shuka*, the only garment he wore, knotted over one shoulder and carrying his spear. He had been attached to a Scottish regiment serving in the Aberdare Forest during the Mau Mau troubles and, therefore, had had some experience with Europeans. We soon got on close terms and I liked him enormously. Once again, I travelled up the west side of the Mathews Range. In 1961 tremendous rains had followed the drought and the country was now very green. In several places in the Mathews and the Ndotos, the mountain-faces had become detached, leaving large precipitous scars. I had never seen the like of this before.

We approached the Milgis luggah travelling through thick scrub country and following a path almost as wide as a road trampled out by elephant. I was wondering where we would find enough space to camp, but late in the evening we came to a large clearing. It was full of elephant, probably more than a hundred. To move them, I fired a shot in the air and the surrounding bush erupted with more elephant trumpeting as they went up the hillside.

The following morning, I decided to travel across the plains below and, by so doing, avoid encountering more elephant at close quarters. We came across another large herd of elephant before getting into more open country. In the afternoon I shot a Grant's gazelle. One of the men with me was a young Boran, a Muslim, and he cut its throat before hanging it on the camel. A short way ahead of us were some large trees, and here was a big pool of water. We camped a hundred yards or more from the pool. In the evening some rhino came down to drink and we chased them away. As usual, I did not put up my tent, which I kept in case of rain, and instead we lay down in a row. Ibach, who had rejoined me, was next to me with the camels couched and hobbled close by. Soon after dark a large number of elephant came down to drink and bathe in the pool. We made up the fire and an hour or two later we were woken by more elephant at the pool. Again we stoked up the fire. Elephant will pass very close to a camp at night but I know of no case where they have deliberately attacked it. However, anybody moving about on foot among elephant in the dark is at considerable risk, since he will probably be unable to see them; they, on the other hand, will be aware of his presence and may regard it as a threat. Shortly after this we realized that there were now some rhino at the pool. I certainly did not want them any closer to us.

Sometime later I was woken again. I thought it was Ibach, who had been snoring, but realized at once that it was a lion. I switched on my torch and saw a large male lion facing me only a few yards away. He immediately turned and made off into the darkness. The others were still asleep. I woke Lokuyie and then, searching round with the torch, we picked up the eyes of two lion. I fired three shots over them, but they paid no attention and continued to move about round the camp for the rest of the night. The gazelle I had shot was hung in a tree immediately above my head and I realized that the lion had probably followed the blood trail and were now trying to drive me off my kill. The others went back to sleep but I sat there with my rifle, on guard, not that I could have done much in the dark. Each time I switched on my torch the beam eventually picked up their eyes.

I must have been half-dozing when suddenly the hobbled camels scrambled to their feet and I thought, 'Damn! The lion have killed one of them.' There was already just a touch of dawn light; alarmingly, the torch showed up a rhino facing me twenty or thirty yards away. I roused the others and we shouted at it. It stood for a moment or two, snorted and then, to our relief, moved off. Soon afterwards, when I was in the Serengeti, I camped beside the Adamsons and the three of us had dinner together. George was sitting next to me and Joy was on the other side of the fire. That evening I described what had happened and ended by saying to Joy, 'Of course, this experience has convinced me that the only rational place for these animals is in Whipsnade.' In a second, she was on her feet, claw-like hands reaching out towards me across the fire as she shouted in her broken English, 'You dare say a zing like zat to me!'

George warned me to shut my tent that night since the night before a lion had come very close to his, and a lion did indeed roar outside my tent. It must have been very close, for I heard the intake of its breath each time it did so. Later, when I was in England, I got a letter from Myles Turner, the assistant park Warden, saying that he thought I might be interested to know that some people had camped in the same place a few days after I had left with the flap of their tent open. One of them who was sleeping near the entrance had been taken out of the tent by a lion which had seized him by the head. His companions had gone in pursuit and the lion dropped him and made off, but the man died shortly afterwards. This lion was one of two. Not knowing which of them had attacked the man, Myles Turner shot them both and, unbelievably, was criticized by some people for doing so.

I am convinced that lion will not become maneaters except on very rare occasions. I have lived on and off for more than forty years in areas of the Sudan and Kenya where lion were numerous. From my own experience I know of only two other cases when a lion has killed, or intended to kill, a human being without provocation. In 1972, one of Rodney Elliott's Game Rangers was carried off in his blanket without serious injury; and in 1993, a lion killed and ate a girl who was herding her goats near here in Maralal and wounded another. All that was left of the dead girl was her head and a foot. Had there been a maneater anywhere in Kutum District while I was there I should most certainly have been asked to come and shoot it. Travelling in the Sudan and Kenya I slept with my companions on the ground in the open and on three occasions lion came within a few feet to investigate us during the night, apparently without any intention of harming us. This suggests to me that wild lion do not regard man as a natural prey.

It would seem to me, from what I have read, that in India tigers take much more frequently to maneating than do lion in Africa. In contrast to India, as far as I am aware, there have been comparatively few maneaters in Africa and then only in certain areas. One such case, of course, involved the notorious maneaters of Tsavo, incidentally eating Indian railway workers.

Among the Samburu until recently dead *moran* were laid out under a tree, covered with leaves and left for the hyenas to eat. This could have provided a meal for any lion in the vicinity had it been so inclined.

I first met George and Joy Adamson at Isiolo in 1960 shortly after my arrival in Kenya and after that continued to hear about Elsa from other people. The story of the domesticated Elsa's return to the wild had been a tremendous success both as a book and a film called *Born Free*. Adamson had now acquired those other lion employed in the film, also intending to return them 'to their lost freedom'. For the film these captive lion had been obtained from zoos and private owners. While wild lion have an instinctive respect for human beings, these lion could have no such feeling. It seemed to me that to turn them loose might be highly dangerous. The lion had inevitably lost their instinctive apprehension of human beings due to their close association with them and, since as cubs they had never been taught to hunt, I felt that Adamson's scheme might turn loose a maneater. I had not expressed my feelings except privately to certain Game Wardens who agreed with me, until after I lunched with Bill Woodley and his wife, Ruth, in the Aberdare Park. On that occasion a plane landed on the nearby airfield and an Englishwoman, Mrs Harthoorn, came in carrying a cardboard box. She said, 'Bill, I've brought you the most marvellous present!' and laid the box on the table. We opened it and saw a small, miserable, listless baby lion. It had been abandoned by its mother and George Adamson had picked it up and sent it to Bill, since he had been ordered not to collect and keep any lion cubs in the Park. He had given it to Mrs Harthoorn to take to Bill so that he could look after it. After she had gone Bill knocked the cub on the head, the best thing he could have done under the circumstances. The incident intensified the growing hostility I already felt for the Adamsons' scheme and the whole wave of anthropomorphic sentiment it had aroused about lion. Had they been confronted by a sick and neglected Turkana baby instead of a lion cub, many Europeans might have said, 'It's shameful how these people treat their children,' and done nothing about it.

I went to Nairobi and expressed my feelings in an interview with the *East African Standard* newspaper. I stated in it that I thought the Adamsons' lion were more dangerous than wild lion and that one or more of them might develop into a man-eater for the reasons I have given. I argued that the Adamsons would have done more for lion had they used the money from their book and film to set up a trapping unit in Nairobi. Such a unit could be immediately contacted by any rancher when a lion appeared on his ranch, where he would justifiably shoot it to protect his valuable cattle. Each year many such lion were shot on ranches like this; some of them could easily have been trapped and released in parks. This would have achieved more for the lion in Kenya than eventually releasing seventeen captive lion, all of which came to a premature end.

Adamson took me up on this and wrote in a letter to the *Standard* that the only thing I knew about lion was shooting them, and that far from being dangerous his lion were acquiring an affection for human beings. One of his lion evinced this shortly afterwards by killing his cook and Adamson shot it while it was carrying off the corpse. This lion, known as Boy, had previously mauled Peter and Sarah Jenkins's eight-year-old son Mark: walking past their stationary Land Rover the lion reached in through the open window and grabbed Mark by the arm. That evening Adamson promised Peter that he would shoot Boy as soon as he saw him, but failed to do so. A little later Boy had alarmed Peter's Game Rangers in Meru National Park by trying to get into their house at night. Adamson was fortunate not to have had his brother Terence among others killed when one of his lion came up unexpectedly and grabbed him by the neck. Another did exactly the same thing

Above Pride of lion
Previous page Maasai woman outside her hut at Olmooti
Below Black-maned lion on wildebeest kill

Lokuyie

Ibach

Maasai elder at Albalbal

Turkana elder north of Lodwar

Above and below Lamu: view over the rooftops and the sea front

Opposite Turkana mother bathing her child near Lodwar

Above In the Suguta valley
Opposite Forest on the top of Mount Nyiru
Below My caravan in the Turkana country

Turkana families on the move

Turkana on the wells at Lokichar

Above Turkana hut and
family between the Suguta
and the Kerio

Right Abakan

Above Part of the wildebeest migration, Serengeti

Opposite Maasai *moran*, Ngorongoro

Right A cluster of spears left by Maasai dancers

Overleaf Maasai *moran* wearing the lion-mane headdress from the lion he had speared

to Adamson's assistant Tony Fitzjohn. A Japanese fashion model staying in their camp had been badly mauled on yet another occasion. Later, to ensure the safety of his camp, Adamson enclosed it with a high wire fence to keep his lion outside it.

Julian Huxley maintained that George Adamson, through his work with these lion, had amassed a great deal of hitherto unknown information about lion. It is interesting, however, that George Schaller in his meticulous study *The Serengeti Lion* quotes the innumerable verbal and printed sources of information his book contains, but few of these acknowledgements are attributed to the Adamsons.

I had long wished to see a Sable antelope, perhaps the most spectacular of all African antelopes including the Greater kudu. In Kenya in the Shimba Hills near the coast to the south of Mombasa there was a small herd of Sable and some Roan antelope. While I was there the Warden told me that they were being decimated by a pride of lion. I said, 'Then, why on earth don't you shoot the lion? After all, this is almost the only place where there are any Sable in Kenya.' He replied, 'If it got about that I had shot a lion in a park, there would be the hell of a row.' This is one of the results of the film *Born Free* and its impact on audiences who know nothing about the realities of African wildlife, but have associated themselves with lion. These same people would rather hear that the last Sable in the country had been killed than that lion had been shot to save them.

CHAPTER FOUR

Camels and Canoes

FROM THE WEST SIDE of the Ndotos, we travelled across open country to the South Horr valley where I had been with Frank Steele the year before, camping in the same place. Owing to the heavy rain, vegetation two foot high had sprung up which we had to clear from among the trees. When we woke in the morning, there was an elephant standing under a tree perhaps thirty yards from the tent. He moved off as we got up. We then worked our way round to the southern end of Mount Nyiru, where we camped at Tum, and from there, accompanied by Lokuyie and two others, I had a stiff climb of perhaps two thousand feet to the plateau on top of the mountain, where there was a magnificent forest interspersed by grassy glades and small streams of running water. As we got above the forest, we passed through a belt of bamboo and then, on the final rise, we were on open ground scattered with everlastings. From here, I could see Lake Rudolf stretching away out of sight to the north. The volcanic ridge with Teleki's Volcano which bounds the southern end of the lake was immediately below us, and south of this was the Suguta Valley which this year lay under a sheet of water resembling another lake. The Samburu regard Mount Nyiru as sacred to N'kai, their god. On the summit a great pile of rocks and branches marks the grave of a famous *laibon* and is constantly added to by passing Samburu. I saw many elephant and buffalo on this plateau which must be one of the most attractive places in Kenya.

Travelling from our camp below the mountain by a rough path, we reached the lake's southern end. Then with difficulty we found a way for the camels through the mass of lava round Teleki's Volcano to the western side of the lake where we camped in the forest by the Kerio.

At Lodwar, David Lambert, the recently-appointed DC, gave me permission – after some hesitation – to travel up the Uganda border past Lokichokio, in a remote area where Uganda, the Sudan and Kenya meet. He lent me five camels so that I could rest mine and sent two of his tribal policemen with me. The country ahead had been heavily raided recently by the Karamojong and Dodoth tribes from Uganda. The previous year the Turkana had carried out a series of counter-raids on these tribes and killed over two hundred of them. In February, the government of Kenya, assisted by Ugandan soldiers, had carried out a semi-military operation to disarm the Turkana and had seized a large number of rifles. As we neared Lokichokio we passed a deserted village with vultures sitting in the trees. Later, a man who had escaped from the village told me that it had been attacked that morning and some men and many women and children had been killed. The same day a messenger arrived with a letter from David Lambert telling me under no circumstances to travel any further up the border. He suggested that I cross eastwards along the southern edge of the Lotikipi swamp to the lake and then down to Ferguson's Gulf, and from there westwards to Lodwar. When Nairobi had heard that I was travelling in this area, they had ordered Lambert to recall me immediately.

On my way to the lake, I met two CID officers who were investigating the scene of a massacre of Turkana by Ugandan soldiers under a man called Idi Amin. I found out later in Nairobi that the Kenya government had demanded Amin's arrest and trial but Sir Andrew Cohen, the Governor of Uganda, had been reluctant to do this since Uganda was then on the verge of independence.

When I reached Ferguson's Gulf the scenery was quite different from what I had previously seen of Lake Rudolf. Here the lake was fringed with acacias, doum palms and grass, and birdlife was abundant. On our way back to Maralal from Lodwar while we were resting at midday, a naked Turkana boy who looked about thirteen, armed with a bow and arrows, came over and joined us from some nearby huts. He announced that he was coming with us. We told him we were going a very long way, but he was insistent. Eventually, Lokuyie said, 'All right, let him come with us'; and we told him to go and inform his mother, which he did. A minute or two later he was back saying he had told her. The child's name was Abakan. He came with us to Lamu and eventually to Ngorongoro in Tanganyika before he returned with us to Nairobi, from where I sent him back to his home.

When we climbed up the steep 1000-foot escarpment from the Rift Valley to Maralal, it was late in the evening. There was a rainstorm while we were climbing and one of the camels slipped, fell all the way down and was killed. It was dark by the time my companions had fetched up its load and sorted things out. I had gone on ahead before I heard the news, so we spent a scattered night and did not join up again until the next morning. Some very helpful Samburu took me to their *manyatta* where I slept.

We allowed the camels to graze in the morning and while I was watching them one of them suddenly galloped flat-out for about a hundred yards and collapsed dead. We could find no reason for this, but wondered if it had been bitten by a snake. None of these Samburu had ever seen a camel before but this did not stop them from cutting it up and eating it. After we had reached Maralal I mentioned the assistance these Samburu had given me to the DC, Roger Hosking, and he rewarded them by waiving their taxes for the year.

At Maralal we camped in the same place as the year before. Jomo Kenyatta had been moved from Lodwar to Maralal and arrived there that day. The town had been cordoned off to avoid the possibility of demonstrations against him by European settlers. On learning of my unexpected arrival in the town, Roger Hosking came over to see who I was and how I had got there. Once reassured, he took me to stay with him in his house.

I planned to travel down the Tana river in dug-out canoes and re-visit Lamu, and Hosking advised me to join the Tana at Mbalambala just downstream from the Meru National Park. I intended to travel with my camels by way of Isiolo until I reached Kora, where George Adamson later established a permanent camp, and to keep Lokuyie, Ibach and Abakan with me when I got there. I had expected to send Abakan back to Lodwar from here, but he insisted on remaining. He was a happy little boy and it was indeed fun having him with us.

When travelling with Frank Steele the previous year in the Ndotos, I had seen a group of about fifteen Samburu boys wearing goatskins dyed black, hanging down from one shoulder. They were dressed like this because they were shortly to be circumcised. About every fourteen years a new group of boys is initiated into manhood by being circumcised, and for the next fourteen years they count as warriors, while the previous age-grade of warriors move up to become junior-elders. Boys were hardly ever circumcised before puberty and in consequence they might be grown men when the next initiation took place, but until they had been circumcised they were still considered children, even if they were in fact grown men.

Of the Kenya tribes only the Luo and Turkana do not circumcise, a ritual operation of great importance to the rest. Today, when the Turkana associate with members of these tribes, the fact that they are uncircumcised can prove a disability. Unruly circumcised schoolboys will taunt a Turkana master by saying, 'You are still only a child, so why should we listen to you?' I have heard some Game Rangers who were with me use these words to an unpopular Turkana sergeant.

Circumcision has no ritual significance for the Turkana; for them it is merely a surgical operation and an increasing number – especially of the young men – are now being circumcised. During the years I acted as an unofficial doctor to the Madan in the Marshes of southern Iraq, I circumcised many boys. They soon found that I could heal them in a few days by using antibiotics. It cost a Turkana 200 shillings to be circumcised in the Maralal hospital, whereas I did it for nothing.

Now as we went down to Archer's Post through Samburu country, we frequently encountered parties of Samburu boys wearing the black skins which they continued to wear for a month after they had been circumcised. When we neared Archer's Post we came to a *manyatta* near the distinctive, precipitous flat-topped mountain of Ololokwe. This was Lokuyie's *manyatta* and he left us there while he went off to find his brother who had recently been circumcised. There was no one about except a few women. We unloaded our camels for the night a short distance from the thorn fence which surrounded the *manyatta*. It was nearly dark when Lokuyie came back with one or two other men. Lokuyie said, 'Don't sleep here, move inside the *boma*. There are lions here which trouble us every night and you'd be safer inside.' However, we were in the middle of cooking our evening meal, so I said, 'Let's put our camels inside the *boma* but let's stay here ourselves.' Every night we had been sleeping on the ground fairly close together, except for one young Boran who was on bad terms with the others and slept by himself a short distance away. In the morning when we woke up we found the tracks of three lion which had prowled round close to where I and my companions had been sleeping, in some places passing between us within a few feet. Lokuyie turned to the unpopular young Boran and said, 'You see, even the lions wouldn't go near you.'

We stayed here the following day and in the evening Roger Hosking turned up and spent the night in our camp. Lion roared round the camp and stampeded the cows from a nearby *manyatta* after killing a calf. There was a lot of excitement as the *moran* rushed out with their spears to drive the lion away.

From here it took us another day to reach Archer's Post, where we crossed the river by the bridge and went on to Isiolo. Since we had come down off the Maralal escarpment we had been travelling north of the Uaso Nyiro through what appeared to me some of the most attractive country I had yet seen on this journey. Flat plains and low, rocky hills covered in places with thickish thorn-scrub; along the dry watercourses large flat-topped acacias, perhaps my favourite tree; the purple-grey of the dry scrub and the pale, silvery-coloured grass; the mountains in silhouette all round the horizon; the faded-blue colour of the distance. We often crossed the tracks of rhino, but they were lying up in the thick bush and I was glad that we encountered none of them. Rhino are unpredictable animals and they could have caused chaos had one of them charged into our line of camels tied head-to-tail.

Geoffrey Hill, who had been transferred to Isiolo from

Lodwar, had arranged to have canoes waiting for me at Mbalambala when I arrived there five days later from Isiolo. I sent the camels back from there. I planned to take with me Lokuyie, Ekwar, Abakan and Ibach, the young Turkana who had accompanied me throughout this journey. There were four dug-out canoes roped together in pairs, with four canoe-men to each pair. The previous evening, little Abakan had declared that he was going back to Lodwar. I told him I could easily have sent him back from Isiolo, but that I could not possibly let him go back from here now that the camels were gone. By now the child was almost in tears, insisting he would go no further. Eventually it emerged that since we had arrived here he had heard frightening stories about hippo attacking boats on the river, but I finally convinced him that I would protect him with my rifle and this reassured him.

My four companions and I travelled in one pair of canoes and my kit in the other pair. We had an eventful first morning. The river was still running high after the year's heavy rain and there was a stiff breeze blowing which sloshed so much water into the canoes that we had to stop and bale them out. We had not gone far down the river when we ran into hippo. On three occasions we were charged by individual hippo, an alarming experience as, open-mouthed, they surged through the water towards us. The first two turned back some distance away but the last really did come very close. When I was on the point of firing, with the others shouting, 'Shoot! Shoot!' it submerged. I hoped it would not come up again under the canoe and turn it over, for none of the boys could swim and there were a lot of crocodiles in the river. We saw more hippo during the eight days it took us to reach Garissa but none of them threatened us. Each day we stopped on a sandbank at midday to cook a meal and again in the evening to sleep. I did wonder whether a crocodile might take one of us while we were sleeping so close to the water's edge, but the canoe-men who were familiar with the river showed no apprehension.

Dense forest lined both banks of the river except in a few places where there was a little cultivation, in many cases just a single hut and a small patch of maize. I became conscious of the ceaseless struggle that went on here against the encroaching jungle and the devastation caused by elephant, hippo, buffalo and other animals. Looking on the scene, I remembered Kipling's story, 'Letting in the Jungle'; a moment's let-up and all traces of man and his work would disappear. Further downstream, on the north bank, wherever the forest became thinner, the Somalis had brought down their flocks and herds to water. Going silently down the river, I saw more hippo and crocodiles and, every now and again, elephant. I had hoped to see many animals coming down to drink, but in fact saw few since in many places the river had overflowed its banks. I did see lots of baboons and the Sykes's monkeys which I had never seen before.

When we got to Garissa I found it was a small town in a district inhabited largely by Somalis with a few thousand of the original riverine tribes surviving here. My canoe-men, who were from these tribes, sang some very attractive songs as they poled and paddled the canoes. I stayed with the DC, Donald Clay, and his wife. At its height, the flooded river had reached right up to the doorstep of their house and had buckled a steel-girder bridge over the Tana. Donald Clay sent back my canoes to Mbalambala and engaged others to take me downstream to Walu, where I planned to hire donkeys from the Somalis to take me through the Boni Forest to Lamu.

During four interesting and useful days with the Clays, I learned a lot about the Somali intrusion into Kenya, and for the first time realized how comparatively recent it had been. The Somalis claim today that much of the NFD had originally been part of Somalia, but this is nonsense. In the past, the Laikipiak Maasai dominated the country even as far north as the Juba River and fought incessantly with the Somalis, usually winning the battle, but losing the war. In 1925 the British agreed to redraw the frontier between Kenya and Italian Somaliland, ceding some territory south of the Juba River to the Italians. Since then the Somalis have encroached continuously on Kenya. The first Somalis to appear in Wajir arrived there as late as 1914 and the Kenyan government would have expelled them by force had they then had sufficient troops at their disposal. When I was in Garissa, the Somalis were confined to north of the Tana River. This no longer applies today.

We left Garissa on 26 June and arrived at Walu five days later. We passed many hippo on our way down the river and, on more than one occasion, when they looked as if they might be aggressive I fired a shot into the water near them, which made them submerge. I remember a place with elephant on one side of the river and buffalo on the other. As I was photographing the elephant, a hippo bumped into the bottom of the baggage-canoe and nearly upset it.

There was a village at Walu and here I hired eight donkeys and engaged four Somalis to go with them. Travelling through the Boni Forest it took us another five days to reach Lamu. I was disappointed by the Boni Forest which I had expected to be tropical and luxuriant; in fact, it consisted largely of endless clusters of doum palms and other uninteresting-looking trees. I had hoped to see Hunter's hartebeest which are entirely restricted to this area of Kenya, but failed to do so, although when he was on his own Lokuyie did apparently see one. Later, when I travelled down here by car, I saw three. Nearly every night we heard lion roaring in the forest and the Somalis were apprehensive about the safety of their donkeys. Recently, while on their way to Lamu, a lion had killed one of their donkeys.

Just before we emerged from the forest I encountered Tony Carn, a young Assistant Game Warden who was engaged there on elephant control. I left my four companions at the settlement on the coast to await my return in two days' time while I sailed with Tony Carn on 5 July across the narrow strait to Lamu. Lamu was as yet unspoilt by the influx of hordes of tourists and it made an interesting conclusion to the long journey which I had just completed. The five of us got a lift back to Garissa on a lorry and from there returned in a bus to Nairobi.

My intention when I came to Kenya had been to make one, possibly two camel-journeys in the NFD. Now I felt that I had seen all I wanted to of the NFD, and consequently of Kenya, since I had no interest in the European settlements in the White Highlands and other parts of the country which I had not as yet bothered to look at. I had enjoyed my visit to Tanganyika and the time I had spent there with John Newbould. Now I was anxious to return there and see more of the Maasai and the country's abundant wildlife. Soon after I got back to Nairobi from Lamu at the end of July 1962, Arthur Bentinck drove me, with Lokuyie and the three others including Abakan, to Ngorongoro where I rejoined John Newbould. Arthur Bentinck had become a close family friend since he had been my father's Military Attaché in Abyssinia in 1917–18 after being badly wounded in France; I envied him for he had been in many remote and exciting areas. I stayed with John for a month, during which he took us in his Land Rover to Seronera. This journey took us through the heart of the Serengeti and we covered a large area and saw a wide variety of animals. Sometimes we saw as many as thirty lion in a day. Both John and I felt separated from our surroundings by being in a car and consequently to some extent frustrated.

From Seronera we now travelled due east to Lake Natron. When we were perhaps a mile from the lake, I began to hear a distant sound almost like an excited crowd at a football match, which grew louder and louder as we approached. On the lake shore and especially on the nearby islands were thousands of pelicans; the greater number of them were immature and as yet unable to fly. We stayed there for an hour or so before we could tear ourselves away from this extraordinary scene. Next day we reached Sale, a Sonjo village. The village, unlike any I had seen before, was surrounded by a defensive wooden stockade. John had been here before and a number of men came out to greet him; they produced some pots of mead for us to drink. This unusual drink was agreeable but potent; little Abakan drank some and became mildly and affectionately intoxicated.

Talking things over when we got back to Ngorongoro, John and I decided to do another proper journey the following year, this time travelling on foot with donkeys southwards across the Maasai Steppe as far south as the Maasai territory extended. When I went back to Nairobi on my way to England, Ibach stayed behind with John at Ngorongoro and in Nairobi I regretfully parted from the others. Ekwar had made himself responsible for seeing Abakan safely back to his home.

CHAPTER FIVE

Across the Maasai Steppe

IN MAY THE FOLLOWING YEAR, John Newbould met me in Nairobi and took me back to Ngorongoro. On our way there we stayed in Arusha with John Owen and his wife. He was now in charge of Tanganyika's National Parks. I had known him in the Sudan before the war when we were both serving there as Assistant District Commissioners. While I was in Arusha I also met Brian Hartley whom I had previously met in southern Arabia. He lent me a heavy rifle for our forthcoming journey.

Before starting on our journey south across Maasailand, we went by car into the Serengeti hoping to see the start of the wildebeest migration. Two million or more wildebeest were reliably estimated to take part in this annual migration which goes as far north as the Maasai Mara in Kenya before turning back. When we caught up with the beginning of this migration, they were still in huge scattered herds all moving in the same direction. Though the wildebeest were moving through bush country I got some impression of the vast numbers of animals involved, which included zebra and gazelle. On our way back to Ngorongoro, we encountered another vast collection of wildebeest in more open country, all drifting northwards, and the same day counted nineteen lion which were following them. The weather had been unsettled and back at Ngorongoro there was a tremendous storm of rain with thunder and lightning.

We started off on 21 June 1963 with fifteen donkeys. With

us we had Ibach and five other men, one of them a Maasai, with all of whom John was well acquainted. At first we travelled for a week across grassy uplands towards the Embagai crater. We camped on the crater's edge by a pool in a forest of hagenia and juniper trees that covered the slopes of the crater. Two Maasai turned up in our camp with a small black-and-white dog resembling a terrier. It immediately came over and joined us and refused to go back to them. They said we could keep it if we gave them a shilling; our men immediately christened it 'Shillingi'. From now on it associated itself entirely with John and myself. Except for our men, it would allow no Africans to approach our possessions, growling at them if they tried to come nearer than four or five yards and attacking them if they did so. We had to warn strangers to keep away.

Throughout this journey we slept on the ground in the open, since we had no tent, and Shillingi kept guard over us. Not infrequently hyenas came close to where we were lying and Shillingi chased them away. I was glad to have him there for I knew of several cases where hyenas had grabbed sleeping men by the face. We tried whenever possible to cut enough bushes to make some sort of *boma* to enclose the donkeys at night and slept downwind of it so that Shillingi would know if any lion or hyenas approached them.

Next morning we went down to the soda lake at the bottom of the crater where there were flamingos and duck, and the following day we climbed to the 12,000-foot summit of the nearby mountain, Loolmalasin. On the march in bush country I went ahead with the heavy rifle and John brought up the rear, sometimes a considerable distance behind. At intervals, Shillingi would race up to the front to see that all was well, stay with me for a bit and then drop back again and rejoin

John. Loaded donkeys travel no faster than about two miles an hour; consequently we seldom covered more than ten or twelve miles a day, since this gave the donkeys time to graze. John also had a rifle and shot for food an occasional Grant's gazelle and impala, or guinea fowl, with his shotgun. After a time the donkeys' slowness exasperated John, so I remarked to him provokingly, 'I suppose you'd rather be in a car?'

There was always something to see. Though there was not the abundance of animal life found in the Serengeti, we did see a few giraffe, oryx, zebra, gerenuk and duiker, and periodically the tracks and droppings of elephant and rhino. John was knowledgeable about the vegetation and gave me much interesting information about the plants, shrubs and trees along the way. Some people had criticized him, saying he neglected his job as a Pasture Research Officer by having too many other interests, especially his interest in the Maasai. We encountered Maasai at intervals and on most days some of them turned up in our camp. Once, when I was some distance ahead of the others, five elephant emerged out of the thick bush on to the track a short distance ahead of me and disappeared into it on the other side. Even though I had hunted elephant in the southern Sudan, I never failed to be impressed by how noiselessly they moved, even when pushing their way through thick cover.

A month after we had left Ngorongoro, we arrived at the Namalulu wells. Here the wells had been excavated to a depth of thirty feet, and, inside, sloping trenches gave the cattle access to the water. The trenches were kept clean; when a cow dropped a pat, someone picked it up and put it on her back so that she carried it out of the well with her. Two days later we arrived at Ngasumet wells. Here, three Maasai stood in a well-shaft drawing water. One stood above the other, the man at the bottom filling a leather bucket and throwing it up to the one above, and so on until it reached a fourth man who emptied the water into a trough for the cattle to drink. These men were naked, except for a skin-covering like a helmet which kept their plaited and ochred hair dry. There were a great number of these wells, and making them must have involved much labour; now only a few of them were in use, but even so it required constant work to maintain them. Other deeper wells in the area, for instance at Kitwi and Makami, involved a four-man lift. In such places a very considerable number of cattle were being watered.

A fortnight later, when we were camped beside a dam, many elephant came down to water. The first herd, including three big bulls, cows and calves, stayed drinking and bathing until sunset. More and more elephant kept arriving and went on doing so until well into the night. We built up a couple of big fires and lying in bed we could just make out their dim, silent shapes drifting past in the firelight.

We were now more or less at the southern limit of the Maasai country. We went south for a few more days before we turned back and here we encountered a group of very unusual people whom the men with us called Wandorobo — a term which is extensively used for hunter-gatherers in Kenya and Tanzania. Maddeningly, I can neither remember nor find in my diary any reference to what they called themselves. They lived on berries and wild honey, and what they shot with bows and poisoned arrows; they kept no animals, not even dogs. They cut out small clearings in dense beds of *Sansevieria*, a tall, green, aloe-like plant with clusters of leaves as sharp as bayonets, from which, by fastening the tops together, they made tiny little shelters. I thought they must be very like the Bushmen of the Kalahari from descriptions I had read, but these people appeared to be taller. Their faces resembled those of Bushmen I had seen in photographs. Some of the girls were apricot-coloured; two fifteen-year-old boys had large projecting buttocks, the characteristic *steatopygia* of the Bushmen; the men had assumed Maasai dress. During the night we spent with the Wandorobo, a lion came close to where we lay and growled angrily at a hyena that was following it.

From here, we went back north to Moshi which we reached a fortnight later, after following the Ruvu, a large river in which there were both crocodiles and hippo. Our journey along the west bank of the Ruvu led through the most attractive country. There were patches of forest with big trees on both banks, and the view across the river with open plains and the Pare Mountains in the distance was spacious. As a result of continuous over-grazing by Maasai cattle, the plains on this side of the river were bare and animals were few in number. We saw oryx, gerenuk, Grant's gazelle and impala; and we frequently crossed the tracks of elephant which had presumably come down to drink each night from distant bush-covered hills.

At Moshi, where we stayed with Hugh Lamprey, John sent back his men with the donkeys to Ngorongoro. Accompanied by Ibach and Shillingi, we motored to Arusha. Shillingi hated the car and never willingly got into another.

I was anxious before I left East Africa to see Zanzibar and intended to fly there from Mombasa.

Tanganyika had been granted independence before I arrived there in May, and, having joined with Zanzibar to form one country, was now called Tanzania. During the time I had just spent in Tanzania, life there appeared to be going on as before and I was certainly conscious of no change.

I was curious to see Zanzibar since it had been the starting point for the major nineteenth-century expeditions that explored East Africa, including those by Burton and Speke, Thomson and Teleki with whose writings I was familiar.

Ibach required a passport, which of course he did not have, to fly to Zanzibar. However, the Immigration Officer was helpful and gave him a temporary pass. Ibach was very good in the bush and first-rate at tracking and spotting game, but in a large town like Mombasa he felt completely lost. I kept him with me in case he got drunk, when it would have required two policemen to hold him.

On the island, I spent a day in the forest searching unsuccessfully for the indigenous red colobus monkeys. But although interested to have seen Zanzibar, I felt no urge to return there.

Having got back to Mombasa I decided, before I left for England, to visit the Tsavo National Park. I stayed for two nights at the Kitani Lodge and travelled round the park in a hired car. I saw briefly a large number of animals comprising many species but, as always from a car, felt totally dissociated from them.

During the next four years I visited a number of countries which I had been anxious to see, travelling on foot in the remotest areas. In Persia in 1964, for instance, I did three journeys: the first was with two mules carrying the kit through the Elburz Mountains from Meshed to the Valleys of the Assassins. I have seldom disliked any people as much as these Persian villagers. We required nothing from them since we carried food for ourselves. All we needed was a roof to sleep on. For this they invariably charged us and once we had to pay for the use of a paraffin lamp. I had with me a Persian, to whom the mules belonged, and a Kurd who spoke Arabic. I would send the muleteer ahead to a village to find somewhere to sleep. Time and again he was turned away. Not once in the course of this journey were we hospitably received, an astonishing contrast with the Arab hospitality to which I was accustomed and the welcome I had received when I had travelled through Kurdistan.

On the second journey, using ponies, I travelled with the Bakhtiari, whom I liked, as they migrated with their sheep from the Zagros Mountains to the coastal lowlands. Finally, I rode camels across the Dasht-i-Lut desert to Yezd. Two policemen were to accompany me on this third journey. When the officer selected them, they protested violently, saying, 'What crime have we committed to be sent across the Dasht-i-Lut?' Their fears proved to be groundless. Almost every night we camped on water after easy marches. I was interested to see a small herd of onager, or wild ass. Despite my protests, the policemen were determined to shoot one of them but their efforts were incompetent and unsuccessful.

In 1965, I returned to Afghanistan where I had travelled in 1956 using pony transport. I did a second journey with porters during which I covered most of Nuristan, one of the first Europeans to have done so; and later I joined Frank Steele in Jordan. Frank had obtained special permission from the Jordanian authorities for us to make a journey to Petra through areas visited only by officials and others on duty. We followed the Wadi Arabah from Tafilch entering Petra from the north, an area which few people visit.

The following year I attended the celebrations in Addis Ababa marking the twenty-fifth anniversary of Haile Selassie's return to Ethiopia in 1941. I then joined the Royalist forces during the Civil War in the Yemen for the rest of that year and the greater part of the next.

Meanwhile, Frank Steele had been posted to the High

Commission in Nairobi and urged me to return to Kenya, which I did in August 1968. I stayed for three weeks with Frank, his wife, Angela, and their two children one of whom, Venetia, is my god-daughter. During this time we went to the coast for a short holiday. I later joined Frank and his son, also called Frank, on a short foot safari, with camels carrying our loads, along the Seiya luggah which runs in the low country between the Lorogi plateau, on which Maralal stands, and the Mathews Range.

In mid-September I returned to Maralal and, having bought six camels from the Rendille, set off from Baragoi. As well as two Rendille camelmen, I had Ekwar, Ibach, Neftali – a young Kikuyu who was energetic, enjoyed travelling and got on with the others – and another young Turkana called Lowassa who cooked for us. Rodney Elliott provided me with a Game Ranger called Longacha. He was a Samburu, authoritative, intelligent and physically powerful. We had a dry march through the Samburu Hills and an exhausting struggle across the Suguta Valley, guided by Longacha through small dunes of soft sand, which took about four hours. When we reached the far side, the others said, 'We will go anywhere else with you, but never again across the Suguta.' I was reassured by this since I had felt quite exhausted, but had attributed this to having had a cartilage removed from either knee before I went on my second journey to the Yemen. There, this had proved a handicap when I had had to squat down as Arabs do to pee.

Sometimes we started to load as early as four in the morning so as to get away at dawn. Lowassa would boil some water to make tea, while the camelmen, helped by the others, fastened the *herios*, the hides and four poles which make up the baggage-saddles of these tribes on to the protesting camels. We usually travelled for about four hours. We would stop

70

whenever it began to get unpleasantly hot or we felt like a rest, for even after the river had dried up there were wells every mile or so in the sandy riverbed, and plenty of shade for us and food for the camels on either bank. Then, if we felt like it, we went on again for another couple of hours in the evening.

We camped next day on the nearby Kerio and travelled slowly down the riverbed through thick forest to Lake Turkana, as Lake Rudolf was now called. At the mouth of the Kerio, dense reed beds prevented us from seeing the lake, but we were just able to glimpse it through the reeds when we reached the nearby mouth of the Turkwel. We followed the Turkwel up to Lodwar. At Lodwar, I found the DC and other African officials both welcoming and friendly, and neither here nor anywhere else in Kenya did I meet with tiresome demands for permits or restrictions of any kind on my journeys. Longacha told me that there was a young Turkana here who had walked up by himself from Loiengalani to join his father who had been serving as a policeman in Lodwar but had since been transferred to Mandera. The boy had been here for some time and knew nobody. Longacha asked if he could come with us to Maralal, from where he would be able to get back to Loiengalani. I told Longacha to fetch the boy and he came back with a naked young Turkana who appeared to be about fourteen. He was a powerfully built, cheerful-looking lad with an engaging smile. I said he could certainly come with us and gave him a few shillings to buy a *shuka*, promising him more when we got to Maralal if he was useful on the journey. He said his name was Erope, which in Turkana means 'spring rains'.

We left Lodwar on 14 October travelling up the bed of the Turkwel. The forest still came down almost to the town. Here the river was dry, but the forest on either side was thick and green from recent rain and, except in a few places, impassable for loaded camels.

I always went on ahead with Ibach and the Game Ranger, who was armed with a rifle. Ibach already showed a remarkable understanding of wild animals. Once he noticed some elephant just visible on a small island in the middle of the river. To move them, so that we could pass, I fired off my shotgun. The herd milled round for a second or two and then scrambled up the bank and disappeared into the forest. A large bull with a smaller bull in attendance remained behind and came forward to face us. The smaller bull then made a demonstration charge towards us before withdrawing to join the bigger bull. Realizing that we should have trouble if we tried to pass them, we turned back down the riverbed looking for a way round them, but the forest was so thick that we had to go back perhaps a mile before we succeeded in doing so. We then had difficulty in getting back through the forest on to the Turkwel. Further up the Turkwel we came on some running water which became more and more abundant as we went upstream until it was two feet deep. Eventually we turned south across bush-covered country by the route we had followed in 1961 and crossed the Kerio.

We had met few Turkana on the Turkwel except for occasional groups of men carrying hide shields, something I had not seen them do before. The country here was in a disturbed state. One group called the Nyoroko, who were troublesome even under British rule, had now acquired some modern rifles from the Sudan and were raiding other Turkana and the neighbouring tribes. The name 'Nyoroko' became synonymous with outlaws. They were also fighting with the Pokot, their traditional enemies. Two months previously this tribe had surprised some Turkana while they were watering their herds on the Turkwel, and killed nine of them, wounding another seven and driving off their cattle, camels and other animals. The Turkana had pursued them and recovered their stock, killing one Pokot. Since then, there had been intermittent raids and I expected the Turkana to stage a big counter-raid before long. When we passed through the Pokot country on our way to Maralal, we found that their warriors, too, were carrying shields as well as spears. In this setting of tribal unrest, my journey could easily have been like one undertaken in the last century.

When I arrived in Maralal on 20 November, Rodney Elliott was still the Game Warden. He bought my camels for the Game Department and arranged to send Erope back to Loiengalani.

After a short stay with Frank and Angela Steele in Nairobi I went back to Tsavo East National Park and felt quite differently about it, for this time I was staying with Phil Glover, a biologist who was there to study the elephant and their habitat. He was a man I liked instinctively and I was fascinated by all he had to tell me; staying with him I now found myself involved in what was going on in the park. He told me it was estimated that there were 20,000 elephant in the park and approximately 8000 rhino. Over the past years, the number of elephant in the park had greatly increased and they had now destroyed large areas of trees, killing them by stripping the bark. One effect of this, however, had been to open up the park to other animals and this made it far easier to see them and Tsavo East consequently more interesting as a park. Like many people, I had believed that the only hope of saving the park was to cull the elephant. Dr Richard Laws among others had estimated that it would be necessary to cull half of them, but the park Warden, David Sheldrick, and Phil Glover had rightly opposed any culling. Phil Glover told me it had been established that when elephant in an area became too crowded the birthrate automatically dropped; and he also pointed out that had elephant been culled as proposed prior to the drought in 1960, which killed a very large number of them anyway, as well as rhino, the park's elephant population would now be severely depleted.

Phil Glover drove me back to Nairobi and this time I stayed with John Seago, brother of Edward Seago, the landscape painter. He and his partner, Tony Parkinson, trapped animals for export to zoos and also for translocation. There were several other animal-trappers in Kenya, but Seago and Parkinson had a reputation that was quite outstanding. I went with them to the Aberdares where Tony Parkinson was trapping bongo, a species of forest antelope. Previously, the few bongo that had been captured had been bayed with dogs, but he had devised an ingenious method by which bongo followed one of their well-used trails until they ended in a carefully concealed enclosure from which they could not escape. John Seago and Tony Parkinson had already captured four, which I saw among their animals in Nairobi. From now on, for many years, John Seago's house became my base whenever I was in Kenya.

Denis Zaphiro, a Game Warden in Kenya, came to dinner one night while I was with John Seago. His father, Philip Zaphiro, had been an almost legendary figure in Kenya where, with a small body of 'Abyssinian scallywags', as they were called, based on Moyale and totally unsupported, he held the frontier for years against Abyssinian intrusion. This in turn had prompted Delamere to make his famous remark, 'Why a Greek?' Philip Zaphiro was transferred in 1912 to my father's staff in Addis Ababa. He had a remarkable gift for languages and spoke virtually all the Abyssinian dialects. My father relied on him as his interpreter and counted on him for local information. I remember him as an endearing figure in the Legation throughout my childhood. He had been appointed Oriental Secretary and awarded a CMG by the time I returned to Addis Ababa for Haile Selassie's coronation in 1930. Denis was then a small child whom I remember fancifully dressed in a kilt. Since then he had been at Rugby School and had served in the Essex Regiment; he had been transferred from the southern Sudan at his request to serve as a Game Warden in Kenya. Shortly after I met him this time, Denis took me to the Mara Reserve. Lynn Temple-Boreham, the Warden, cautioned us before we went there, 'For God's sake, if you see the tracks of another car don't follow them or you'll turn it into a road.' We were there for four days and only on the last day saw another car. I shall always be glad that I saw the Mara when I did, while it still remained an unspoilt paradise of African wildlife.

CHAPTER SIX

Journey to Alia Bay

I RETURNED AGAIN TO KENYA in 1969, drawn once more by the lure of the NFD and the desire to travel with my companions of the previous year. When Kenya became independent in 1963 the NFD had been abolished and incorporated into the new provinces of the Rift Valley and the Eastern Province.

When I arrived in Nairobi in early July I bought a Land Rover. All my life I have resented cars and aeroplanes, realizing that they must eventually rob the world of all diversity. By 1969 to a large extent this had already happened, even though mass-tourism was still to come. My contemporaries at school had one and all been fascinated by cars. I had no wish to know anything about them, a feeling I still have today. However, I had learned to drive by the time I went to Oxford. Some years earlier my mother had bought a car. Previous to that, our only means of transport had been a pony-trap. We bought a Baby Austin and I had learned to drive this in 1928 in order to make myself and my brothers independent. Though I had never owned a car, I felt that I must now buy one for myself in order not to be dependent upon others to take me to the starting points of my journeys in Kenya. To this day, travelling in a vehicle, especially in remote areas, I feel thwarted. Most of my travels have been in areas of the world that had never even heard an engine.

I drove to Maralal in my new Land Rover and from there to Ilaut where I spent a week haggling with the Rendille over camels. In the end I got the seven I required, but only with difficulty and at high prices. A camel then was worth three to four hundred shillings. They were asking nine hundred, came down to seven hundred and then took their animals away. Not many camels were offered for sale and in the end I got mine for almost five hundred shillings each.

In Nairobi, Maralal and Baragoi I had now collected the same party who were with me the previous year: Ibach, Ekwar, Lowassa, Neftali and Longacha. At Baragoi we used the same pleasant campsite as before, about a mile from the town and down by the edge of the luggah. We were there for three days and on the second day, the Father who ran the Catholic Mission came down and invited me to supper; a friendly, rotund little man, he seemed glad to have a visitor. After that he made a habit of coming down the hill to fetch me whenever I was in Baragoi. Before leaving Baragoi I left my Land Rover with the Mission.

We left for Loiengalani on 20 August, camping at South Horr on the second day and arriving at Loiengalani five days later. As we approached Lake Turkana, to the east I saw again the faint, cleft outline of Mount Kulal on the skyline beyond a vast jumbled desolation of lava. The only vegetation was an occasional small leafless bush and patches of withered yellow grass in a dry watercourse or two running down to the lake. The vivid blue water stretched to the black Turkana mountains on the far side.

As we neared Loiengalani, Erope popped out of a bush, and said, 'I'm coming with you!' I said at once, 'Good, come with us', which he did; and he was to remain with me for nine years.

At Loiengalani the wind was as violent as ever. When I had visited Loiengalani with Frank Steele in 1961 it had been an attractive empty oasis of doum palms and acacia trees in the surrounding desolation. Now a Catholic Mission station had been built on the very spot where we had formerly camped and, on the insistence of the Mission, the once-naked people were now wearing an incongruous assortment of clothes. As well as the Mission and a lodge, there were a few rudimentary shops nearby and scattered clusters of simple Turkana huts. A number of El Molo, a small fishing community, had drifted into the town from their settlement further up the lake.

An enterprising Seychellois with his wife and two small children had taken over and enlarged the two buildings beside the pool and converted them into a lodge. Some years later, when my friend the priest from Baragoi and his Italian driver were staying there, three Shifta armed with rifles turned up after dark, fired a shot or two into the engine of their lorry, then entered the lodge and shot the Seychellois and the missionary from Baragoi. They took the driver outside, partially flayed him and killed him when he failed at their orders to start the damaged lorry. Sometime after this, Rodney Elliott told me that once when he was staying there he had advised the Seychellois to keep his rifle handy at night rather than in the safe. However, the man preferred to keep it in the safe, saying that if it were stolen there would be endless trouble with the police. Rodney had said, 'Well, I can see what will happen if Shifta do turn up. You'll shout to your servant, "Bring the key of the safe! Hurry, bring the key of the safe!", and he'll say, "Bwana, you've got it in your room", and that'll be that.' Mercifully, on the night the Shifta did come, the wife and children of the Seychellois were in Nairobi. There has been much speculation as to the motive for this murder but no satisfactory answer. Indeed, it is not even known who did it.

*   *   *

Entry to the NFD had formerly been forbidden by the British to all others than government officials and those with special permits; Jomo Kenyatta had maintained this restriction for a year or two after independence. This was originally due to the risk of raids by large and powerfully armed bands of Ethiopians, as described by Major Rayne in *The Ivory Raiders* and by Major Henry Darley in his book, *Slaves and Ivory*; constant raids were also carried out by tribes from Ethiopia across the frontier, which continue even today. In 1961 when Frank Steele and I met Peter Walters, the Provincial Commissioner in Isiolo, he had warned us to be on the lookout for raiding parties from Ethiopia and said, half-jokingly, 'If you see anyone up there, you'd better shoot them. They will have no right to be there anyway.' As a matter of fact when we had travelled there the area was quiet. This time, however, when I revisited Loiengalani everyone seemed nervous and on edge, and rumours of raids by the Merille and Boran from across the frontier were rife.

These raids were largely carried out by the Merille who inhabited Ethiopian territory where the Omo River enters Lake Turkana, and by Boran who lived further east across the frontier in Ethiopia. Many of the Boran, a large powerful tribe of the Galla, or Oromo as they are now called, escaped southwards into Kenya to avoid being ruled by the Ethiopians. The Ethiopian government demanded their return and in 1913 my father had trekked from Addis Ababa to Nairobi to meet the Governor and discuss this and other problems. I read somewhere in one of his letters that he had said to the Governor, 'While I agree that anybody would be reluctant to return these people to an administration as brutal as that of the Abyssinians, I do feel that it might be to the ultimate advantage of British East Africa to do so.' A considerable number of these Boran refugees were allowed to remain and were allocated territory which had hitherto been occupied by transitory tribes in Kenya. Today, the enormous number of well-armed Somali refugees presents Kenya with an appalling problem.

Organized raids by the Ethiopians were things of the past; however, tribal raids, mostly by the formidable Merille or Gelubba inhabiting Ethiopian territory immediately north of Lake Turkana, and by Boran from across the frontier, were still frequent. There was also inter-tribal hostility in the district. The Turkana were blood-enemies of the Merille; the Samburu and Rendille were hostile to the Boran.

We left Loiengalani on 29 August, travelling on the east side of the lake in order to reach Alia Bay. A week later we encountered a few Rendille. They told us that some thirty Merille, nearly all of whom were armed with rifles, had been seen here about a month previously. They warned us that the country north of here had been evacuated and we could only expect to meet raiders there. Two days later, my companions were alerted by the week-old tracks of one man and the following day the week-old tracks of another man. Merille raiders send out six or more scouts to locate a target, then raid it when the moon is more or less full so as to be able to drive the captured stock as far as possible under cover of night. They endeavour to kill everybody in the encampment to avoid the possibility of anyone escaping and spreading the alarm.

On the same day as we met the Rendille we had to leave the lakeshore at Moiti and go inland to avoid a low ridge which ran into the water. Just before sunset we arrived at Alia Bay and camped under some acacia trees near a marsh with reeds and *ambach* fringing the lake. Mosquitoes were bad that night. Since leaving Loiengalani we had travelled across generally undulating, shadeless country with occasional lava ridges, luggahs fringed with thin bush and patches of thicker bush. We had seen a lot of animals: as many as seventy Beisa oryx in one day, many Grevy's zebra and Grant's gazelle, and increasing numbers of topi, 152 on the last day's march. We had also seen occasional gerenuk and giraffe, one hippo and a large number of ostriches. We had noticed the tracks of a rhino, in several places the tracks of lion and once the tracks of a leopard. That night, we saw some lights in the far distance. We stayed for two days at Alia Bay before setting off in a south-easterly direction for North Horr. On the first day's march we crossed the tracks of six men. After a further two days' march over stony, volcanic country we camped on water for two days in a very pleasant spot under some acacia trees in a small luggah. Here were tracks of a number of rhino and many lion. There were many guinea fowl and I shot a lot of them to feed us.

We carried rice, white flour to make chapattis for myself, tins of tomato purée – the only tinned food I carried – maize-flour or *ugali* to make *posho* for the others, a large quantity of sugar and plenty of tea, salt, ghee and onions for all of us. We bought a goat whenever possible, and I shot an occasional Grant's gazelle besides guinea fowl and sandgrouse. All I had to drink was tea and water flavoured sometimes with powdered lemon. The water of Lake Turkana, though drinkable, tastes unpleasantly brackish. At intervals on the journey, as here, we had found fresh water to drink.

As we approached North Horr over a bare gravel plain we encountered Turkana and Boran herdsmen with their flocks of goats, the first people we had seen for almost a fortnight. At North Horr we camped on a low sandhill under an acacia tree. It was a desolate sort of spot with only a police post and a scattering of huts. One of my two Rendille camelmen wandered off, came back blind drunk, threatened Ekwar with a spear, and had to be locked up for the night by the police.

We set off next morning, travelling south-west for six hours, stopped for the night, started again before sunrise and three and a half hours later arrived at the shallow wells at Gus where there was a grove of doum palms. A police lorry carrying a Boran elder arrived from Marsabit with rations for the police at Loiengalani. The elder had come to warn the Boran that a large force of Merille had passed Alia Bay in three bands, numbering in all some 250–300 men, one of these bands heading for Moiti. He suggested that the tracks of the six men we had seen near Alia Bay had probably been made by their scouts. Our camp that night was surrounded by hyenas and in the morning Lokichar estimated from their tracks that they had numbered more than twenty. They had been very noisy during the night. To me, the whooping cry of a hyena, ever since my childhood has been the sound of Africa, even more than the roar of the lion.

We reached Lare Dabach two days later. The going was difficult as we travelled south for three hours over some old lava flow from Kulal, the country strewn with lava weathered into a chaos of boulders. The following day we struggled on over lava ridges and then across a stony plateau. The vegetation here was sparse, one or two leafless acacias and a few whistling thorns. Each day we saw an occasional oryx. Early the next morning we arrived at Lare Dabach, a pleasant, sheltered valley where there was a shallow stream of clean fresh water flanked with doum palms and large acacias. From here I had a good view of the nearby northern half of Mount Kulal. I sent Erope, Ekwar and Neftali with a camel to replenish our *posho* at Loiengalani, which was no distance from here. They rejoined us at Mouwoligiteng two days later. Here I remember quite vividly that I camped under a large acacia whose spreading branches hung down all round my bed almost like a tent. This was a delightful spot and the most attractive campsite on this journey. There was a large pool of fresh water and Longacha, the Game Ranger, maintained, despite my disbelief, that it held a few small crocodiles. We stayed here for two days and Turkana arrived at intervals to water strings of goats. Clouds of sandgrouse flew in to drink at sunset.

With Longacha, Erope and Lowassa I spent the second day exploring the Larachi Gorge which divides the 7,500-foot Mount Kulal. From a distance this gorge appears to split the mountain into two equal halves; a volcanic eruption had left a wall of rock which cut the gorge in two but joined the two halves of the mountain. This wall of rock, level with the summit, was so narrow at the top that it has only once been crossed, in 1983, by a party of mountaineers from Nairobi.

It took us three hours over some very rough going to get to the gorge. The sides of the gorge were steep, in places sheer, with euphorbia on the high slopes and forest trees growing in the bottom of the gorge beside a small stream of clear, very cold water. After we had turned back and were approaching the entrance to the gorge, we saw two Samburu *moran* fetching water in a calabash from the stream. On seeing us, they started to run but Longacha shouted to them to stop which they eventually did. They told us that they and three others were eating a Turkana bull in the forest. The other three panicked when they saw us approaching and vanished into the forest, but came back after the two with us had shouted to them and reassured them. Samburu *moran* live almost entirely on meat, milk and blood for the fourteen years that they are *moran* and, above all, they may never eat in the presence of women.

The *moran* in those days were physically very fit and capable of great endurance; for instance, when throwing up buckets to one another to water their cattle at the wells, which they would do for hours on end. I would have thought that this diet of meat, milk and blood would have lacked some essential vitamins. Nowadays, their diet has changed and many of them eat *posho* regularly as well as other food. In those days it was an insult to call a *moran* a *'posho' moran*.

Given a chance any of them would lift a bull and eat it in some secluded place, as these had done. They had killed this bull and were roasting it. We joined them, ate some of the meat and left them to eat the rest. They had kept no look-out so evidently did not expect to be followed, hence their panic on seeing us. We got back to camp late in the evening. We had seen the tracks of a leopard and five Greater kudu. Kulal is one of the few places in Kenya where Greater kudu are to be found. Longacha had seen a kudu bull the previous day.

Having seen this side of the gorge I was interested in its contrast with the other side, known as El Kajarta. This I had seen in 1961, during my journey with Frank Steele on our way to Marsabit, when we had camped near the mouth of the gorge at its eastern end. Then we had penetrated some way up the gorge, which on that side was boulder-strewn with little vegetation, but we had been deterred from going further when we came on the fresh tracks of rhino. Neither of us had any wish to be charged in that confined space.

Still travelling south, parallel with the western side of Kulal, we encountered some difficult lava country where we wasted a lot of time. There were fissures in the lava which we had to circumvent since the camels refused to step across them. On the first night we camped beside a leafless tree in a narrow valley on the southern slopes of Kulal. After this punishing march we rested our camels the following day. We then got back into bush-country comprising *Commiphora*, euphorbia and acacia, and here we found the tracks of more Greater kudu, many lion and a leopard. Two days later, we reached Balesa Kulal. On the way there we saw a few giraffe, two Greater kudu, the tracks and scrapings of several rhino and, in one place, trees which had been damaged by elephant. I fired a shot at some guinea fowl and this disturbed a large lion which had been lying up in some bushes.

That night, one of the Rendille somehow sensed a lion close by, although the man was lying with his head under a blanket. He woke Longacha who saw a lion some twenty yards away. It remained nearby, its eyes shining in the torchlight, until I fired a shot over its head when, with a grunt, it made off. Next morning, the tracks showed that the lion had returned and had lain there downwind, some forty yards off, watching our camp. The camels, however, had not been disturbed.

We moved only a short distance next morning since this was attractive country and there was no reason to push on. Kulal was now behind us. On the right, the jagged peaks of Ol Doinyo Mara were dominated by the long, level summit of Nyiru rising up behind them and, to the east, the distant outline of Marsabit. There seemed to be lion everywhere in this country; one of them disturbed our camels while they were grazing. We dawdled along for several days and on one occasion, during a midday halt, Longacha, Ekwar and Lowassa took the shotgun and went off to shoot guinea fowl. They eventually fired a shot. This alarmed Rendille in a distant group of *manyattas* who thought it must have been fired by Nyoroko or Boran. Their *moran* immediately collected and set off in a body to investigate. Lowassa had meanwhile separated from the others and when he saw these warlike *moran* approaching, he immediately took to his heels. The *moran* raced in pursuit but Lowassa managed to reach Longacha and Ekwar before they overtook him. Longacha then explained to the excited *moran* who they were and they came with him to where we had halted. There must have been at least thirty of them.

We arrived at the Moran luggah, a particularly large, dry watercourse with dense bush on either side, which winds down off Nyiru and from there east, dividing the South Horr hills from the open plains that stretch to Baragoi. Here we saw elephant and the tracks of many rhino. We also saw three male Lesser kudu; this bush country is a favourite haunt of theirs. We followed the luggah for two hours, then camped by a deserted *boma* on the plains and reached Baragoi the next day.

CHAPTER SEVEN

Anti-poaching Safaris

I COLLECTED MY CAR from Baragoi and motored to Maralal on 7 October 1969 where I stayed with Rodney Elliott. Frank Steele and a friend of his, Richard Dearlove, were to join me there ten days later. I planned to travel back to Wamba by way of Barsaloi, the Milgis luggah and the east side of the Mathews Range. Meanwhile, Rodney Elliott was anxious for me to get news of Somali Shifta who were said to be poaching in the area and to shoot them if possible. As well as Longacha, he arranged for five more armed Game Rangers to accompany me with the necessary camels.

These five Rangers were to go on ahead to Barsaloi, collect more camels and join us at Laitagwa, a small village with a couple of shops at the south-western end of the Ndotos. I left my car at Maralal from where, on the return of Frank's car in which we drove to Baragoi, Rodney Elliott would arrange for both cars to be sent to Wamba on 31 October.

With Frank and Richard Dearlove I motored from Baragoi to Masigita where I had arranged for Longacha to rejoin us. From there Frank sent his car back to Maralal. For Richard Dearlove this was a new experience, travelling on foot with camels and not in a car, one which during the ensuing days he appeared to enjoy. I, of course, was delighted to be travelling like this once more with Frank.

At Laitagwa the five Game Rangers joined us with their four camels from Barsaloi. The Milgis, a very large luggah, perhaps as much as two hundred yards in width, passes through the gap between the Ndotos and the Mathews Range; it is formed by the confluence of the Seiya and Barsaloi luggahs. The shallow banks are more or less bare on either side. When we got there after a short march from Laitagwa we found such water as had reached the surface in places mildly brackish. We cast about looking for something better and in a deep elephant's footprint I found fresh water. Before we set off soon after sunrise we saw buffalo and elephant watering in the luggah. We followed the Milgis luggah eastwards for two days through broken, eroded country with scattered bush. On the way, we had frequently seen elephant, rhino, buffalo and the tracks of many lion, as well as giraffe, oryx, Grevy's zebra, gerenuk and a wildcat. Twice, having been warned that there were Shifta in the area, we had been on the alert. In several places, we had seen tracks and other signs, including an abandoned camp and a worn-out shirt left hanging on a tree, but all these signs were more than a week old. On our route we had passed several abandoned *manyattas*. Once we had seen smoke from a burning *manyatta* and had stalked it in case we should find Shifta, but there were none.

With Frank, Richard Dearlove, Longacha, another Game Ranger and Erope we reconnoitred the forest track to the Murit Pass but saw no sign of Shifta. It would have been pleasant to have crossed the pass and gone down to Kichich, where in 1961, on our journey to Lake Rudolf, Frank and I had camped. However, we had to return to our camp and camels on the east side of the Mathews. Kichich was then a superb camping site, a meadow of open ground where buffalo grazed, enclosed by the magnificent forest reaching up the mountainside with a stream of clear, cold water running by in which there were small barbel. Since then this area has been acquired as a permanent commercial campsite, which I resent.

For the next two days we continued southwards down the east side of the Mathews Range until we reached the El Kanto Pass; Wamba lay on the far side of it. We stopped below the Pass and fired a shot or two at guinea fowl which alerted two Samburu who assumed these shots were fired by Shifta and hurried to Wamba to give the alarm. The Assistant Game Warden, some armed Game Rangers, and a platoon of a special police unit, the GSU, and Samburu *moran* arrived in our camp, fortunately taking care to identify us before they started shooting. We crossed the low El Kanto Pass and entered Wamba. The two cars arrived the next day and Frank and Richard Dearlove went straight off in their car to Nairobi. I followed them later in mine.

When I arrived in Nairobi, I stayed again with John Seago; the following morning when he was going downtown in his car, I asked him to take Lowassa, Neftali and Erope with him to see the town, which they had never seen before. He came back later and said that they had lost Erope. John had put the three of them out near the New Stanley Hotel and told them he would come back shortly and pick them up; when he came back only Lowassa and Neftali were waiting there. They said they had left Erope at the corner where John had put them down, told him to stay there and to watch out for John while they went into a shop across the street. When they came back to join him, Erope was gone. I was very worried for Erope was just fourteen years old, spoke only Turkana, had never been in any town other than Lodwar and, I felt, would be hopelessly lost in a city of this size. I immediately got in my car and set off to look for him.

I went down to the New Stanley hoping to find him there.

I searched for him everywhere, without success. Two hours later, John met me outside the New Stanley. I said to him in despair, 'I've hunted everywhere and I can't find him anywhere.' John said, 'Don't worry, he's back in the house and drinking tea.' Apparently, while Erope was waiting for John, a shopkeeper had become suspicious of him and said, 'If you hang about outside my shop, I'll hand you over to the police', so Erope had walked straight back to John's house in Westlands, a distance of perhaps seven miles. Instead of following the indirect route by the main road which John had taken, he had gone back there almost in a straight line through the town. When Neftali asked him what he would have done if he had not found John's house, Erope replied, 'I would have walked back to Loiengalani', and I am sure that he would have got there.

Erope hated cars and would never get into one if he could avoid it. Later, when I was based in Maralal, he would sometimes disappear and when I asked where he was I would be told that he had gone off to see his grandmother at Marsabit. Since he would never contemplate getting a lift in a car, I knew that he would be going on foot and I could not expect to see him back for the best part of a month. I remember on one occasion when my car broke down, he gave it a kick and said, 'Now you can't even eat it!' On the other hand, even as a boy, he was absolutely at home in the bush and he accompanied me everywhere. When I was later doing foot patrols in what is now Meru National Park, senior Game Rangers who were with me would refer to him and seek his advice.

In August 1970 I motored to Maralal. Rodney Elliott had arranged for me to become an Honorary Game Warden and he wanted me now to patrol the Uaso Nyiro River, both upstream and downstream, from Archer's Post where Somali poachers were active. He lent me a .30-06 magazine rifle with a telescopic sight. Before doing so, I went to Garba Tula to buy camels. The Boran produced a succession of decrepit animals, some of them blind in one eye, but after several days of haggling I got six elderly but serviceable camels for a total of just over two thousand shillings.

I stayed with the young Game Warden, Tony Carn, and his wife Velia at their house just outside Isiolo where I camped on the lawn. I had met Tony Carn eight years previously in the Boni Forest after my journey down the Tana River in 1962. Their house and all their possessions had recently been burnt when a calor-gas cylinder exploded in the kitchen at night. Fortunately, the Carns were not there at the time otherwise they would almost certainly have been burned to death. As it was, their dog was burned.

On 16 September I set off up the Uaso Nyiro with six Game Rangers and Erope, Ekwar and Lowassa who were still with me. With the consent of the Samburu, Rodney Elliott had established a game reserve upstream from Archer's Post, where an attractive lodge had now been built on the north bank overlooking the river. Here, for the first and only time, I met up with Richard Leakey, son of Dr Louis Leakey, the eminent palaeontologist who had become internationally famous for his excavations at the Olduvai Gorge in Tanzania.

Some years later the President, Daniel Arap Moi, appointed Richard Leakey as Director of the Kenya Wildlife Service with the specific task of controlling the poaching of elephant in Kenya. Elephant-hunting by the Wagiriama, the Waliangulu and other tribes on the coast, using poisoned arrows and very powerful bows, had been a feature of life there probably for centuries. They had traded the ivory to Arabs who exported it in their dhows; but recently, owing to the enormous increase in the price of ivory, poaching in Kenya was threatening the very existence of elephant in the country. Somali poachers using readily available semi-automatic weapons had now moved in, their activities facilitated by rich and influential Somalis resident in the country.

In the Samburu district in the 1960s, elephant had been abundant and were to be found even as far north as Mount Kulal. Now, encouraged by the Somalis, even the Samburu sometimes killed elephant with their spears. As a result elephant were either killed or driven out of the district into the farmlands to the south. There they were safe but on some ranches they eventually destroyed almost all the wire fences.

Backed by the President, Richard Leakey took immediate and drastic action, which proved effective. In the Samburu district, this had been evinced by the drift back of elephant from the ranches in the south. Today they have reoccupied the country as far north as the Milgis. Sadly, none are yet to be seen at South Horr where, until recently, they were a feature of the landscape. Now at night a herd of perhaps fifty or more elephant frequently moves down the valley through the acacia trees, just below Laputa's house near Maralal where I am living.

Richard Leakey was with Peter Jenkins, the Game Warden in Meru National Park, and his wife Sarah, whom I now met for the first time. The Jenkinses invited me to spend Christmas with them. I continued my patrol the next day and went up on the south side of the river as far as the gorge known as Crocodile Jaws, before returning to Isiolo three weeks later. The river was about thirty yards wide, three feet deep at the crossings, in some places sluggish, in others fast-flowing, and there were deep pools with hippo and some crocodiles in them.

River crocodiles, unlike lake crocodiles, are generally dangerous. In one place, we came upon three crocodiles eating the remains of a baby elephant speared by Samburu; elsewhere we found a large giraffe which had been killed by a lion, lying on a slope at least twenty yards from the river. Crocodiles had been eating it.

Sometimes the river banks were lined with doum palms, or with Tana River poplars and acacias. Away from the river, on both banks, the plains were sometimes bare except for salt bushes, but more generally were covered with scattered thorn scrub, with large acacias along the dry watercourses. Some distance from the river, on either side, were the outlines of mountains; some flat-topped like Ololokwe, others rising in jagged peaks. We often saw herds of elephant bathing in the river, buffalo on its banks and occasional rhino, most often on the plains where there were many other animals. In one day we saw three cheetah, a leopard, six lion, seventy-six giraffe and almost three hundred Grevy's zebra, as well as gerenuk and waterbuck.

We turned back at Crocodile Jaws at the base of the Lorogi Plateau and reached Isiolo seven days later. On one occasion we found a small, abandoned Shifta encampment with the remains of a giraffe which the Rangers estimated these poachers had killed almost a fortnight earlier; on another, we found the four-day-old tracks of seven poachers.

Denis Zaphiro, the Game Warden, had planned to come with me downstream as far as Chanler's Falls and we had agreed he should join me at the Carns' house at Isiolo on 11 October. Meanwhile the Carns were away on local leave and I had about a fortnight to wait before Denis Zaphiro arrived. I spent some of this driving up to Marsabit with Erope and one of the Game Rangers. We spent three days searching the forest for Ahmed, the famous bull elephant which lived there, the successor to several other heavily-tusked elephant of the past; Ahmed's tusks were probably the heaviest now to be found anywhere in Africa. Ahmed used to hang about the edges of the forest and was quite easy to see, but now that a road had been built he had retired to the thicker forest. Eventually, I saw him, having spent the entire day searching for him in the forest. He came out into the open and crossed a stream directly in front of us, giving a fine uninterrupted view of his magnificent, long, thick, inward-curving tusks.

On 17 October, I started off down the Uaso Nyiro from Archer's Post accompanied by Denis Zaphiro and nine Game Rangers, three more than I had had with me previously, since here we were more likely to encounter armed bands of Somali poachers. We had arranged that Frank Steele would meet us at Chanler's Falls, bringing Tony Carn with him. Tony would then take Denis Zaphiro back in Frank's Land Rover to Isiolo, leaving Frank to continue the anti-poaching patrol with me.

We went slowly down the river, the camels doing perhaps four hours a day, which gave us ample time to approach and look at any animals that interested us. On one occasion, we walked over towards some sheer cliffs to get a closer view of a Martial eagle; above the cliffs, vultures were circling and the ledges where they presumably nested were splashed white with their droppings. Erope, who carried my shotgun, had become a good shot and we would send him off to shoot guinea fowl; sometimes he crossed to the far side of the river. Before leaving Isiolo, there had been a very heavy downpour and, as is always the case in these parts, the arid countryside turned green almost overnight and soon afterwards flowers, some white and others yellow, with their strong, sweet scent, came out on the acacias. A variety of small, beautiful flowers

Previous page Mouwoligiteng water hole under the west side of Mount Kulal

Above left Erope

Above right My anti-poaching patrol near Chanler's Falls

Left Erope on patrol

Opposite Ololokwe

Overleaf Mount Kenya

Kisau

Lawi

Elephant killed by poachers' poisoned arrows

Above A Samburu woman building her hut
in a *lorara*, the circumcision encampment

Right Samburu mothers shaving the heads
of their sons on the eve of circumcision

Below Samburu boys in black goatskin
cloaks prior to circumcision

Intiates chanting the *lebarta* (circumcision song)

Opposite Circumcised boy with bow and blunted arrow

Above A Samburu shooting a blocked arrow into the jugular vein of a cow in order to collect its blood

Right Circumcised boy with the birds he has shot hanging down the nape of his neck

Left A Samburu *moran* being decorated by another

Opposite Women and girls at the celebration

Below Meat roasting over pit fires during the final circumcision ceremony of the casting away of the arrows

Traditional dance by *moran*

The new *moran* chanting and dancing

appeared here and there in the grass; but here on the Equator they never provided an effect of massed colour such as I had seen covering the mountain slopes of Kurdistan in spring.

The Game Rangers and Denis caught quite a number of fish which, together with guinea fowl and an occasional Grant's gazelle I shot for meat, helped to vary our food. There appeared to be several different kinds of catfish in the river and the Game Rangers' corporal got the spine of a catfish into his finger. This catfish had a poisonous spine on either side and one on its dorsal fin; as a result the corporal was in great pain for several hours. Some of these catfish were very large, large enough to break our fishing lines.

The game here had been heavily poached and, in contrast to the animals I had encountered on my earlier journey upstream, were very wild.

We had had no more rain since leaving Archer's Post and did not bother to put up a tent. I invariably slept on the ground with the brilliant tropical stars on the move above me. We had passed the tracks of many lion and most nights we heard them roaring, sometimes quite close to the camp. One night they had come especially close; at dawn, Erope made some realistic lion-prints with his fist, a foot or two from the head of the unpopular Game Ranger corporal who was still asleep under his blanket. When the corporal got up and saw them he exclaimed, 'Great God, look at that!' and was laughed at by the others. He never forgave Erope for doing this.

On 24 October, Frank Steele and Tony Carn arrived at Chanler's Falls. Tony Carn wanted to get our news and brief the Game Rangers for the next stage of the journey. Frank had brought some more rations for us. Tony Carn and Denis Zaphiro then left for Isiolo and the same day Frank and I crossed the Uaso Nyiro and camped above the falls on the other side of the gorge. The river was notorious for its crocodiles.

The falls were of no great height but were an unexpected feature in this flat country. We travelled downstream through bush country towards Merti, a lava plateau on our left running parallel with the river, and the going became hard on our camels' feet.

We camped for three days near Merti where we patrolled the surrounding country. Both here and on the way from Chanler's Falls we saw small herds of elephant and also of buffalo. We had come across two rhino that the poachers had shot and in one place the day-old tracks of three Shifta going north from the river, following the tracks of another rhino. We had no water with us so we could not follow them. From the tracks it was evident that rhino were numerous in this bush country. When we arrived at Merti we found two lion on a Grevy's zebra which they had just killed, and another lion nearby.

Tony Carn arrived on 4 November and took Frank back with him to Isiolo. Tony had told me that the wells at Kom Galla were a favourite hideout for poachers in the area and we therefore turned back in their direction. By chance, we encountered a Boran who offered to guide us to Kom Galla since none of the Game Rangers was certain of its location. I therefore employed him as an extra camelman. In several places on our way there we noticed the tracks of small groups of poachers. None of these, however, was recent.

Rodney Elliott had told me that if we did encounter Shifta, who were utterly ruthless, we should shoot them on sight. I had been hoping on this journey that we should do so. At Kom Galla, we left the camels some distance away and approached the wells prepared to fight if we met anybody there; but to our disappointment we failed to do so. Four days later, at Kauro, we were again disappointed not to find any Shifta and only their stale tracks.

CHAPTER EIGHT

Meru, Mount Kenya and the Merille

I NOW TOOK UP the Jenkinses' offer to spend Christmas with them in Meru National Park and had Erope, Kibo, a sixteen-year-old Turkana, and friend of Erope's, and Lowassa with me. Peter had asked me if I would care to stay on and patrol the park for him and I jumped at the offer, for it always frustrated me in a park to be restricted to travelling in a vehicle. Now I should have the whole of this park at my disposal, be able to travel anywhere I wished on foot and spend the night wherever I chose.

After I left Isiolo, Rodney Elliott had taken over my camels with Ekwar who remained at Maralal to look after them. On my way to Meru to the Jenkinses I stayed again with John Seago in Nairobi. While I was there I had taken Erope, Lowassa and Kibo to an amateur boxing match between Kenya and the Soviet Union. Before they really understood what was going on, Erope said, 'If somebody did that to me, I'd kill him.' But when they had grasped the point of it, they became enthusiastic and talked of nothing but boxing for some time. Unlike Lowassa or Kibo, Erope said that he wanted to learn to box so that he could box for Kenya. Erope became the first of my followers whom I did teach to box.

I had a very pleasant Christmas with the Jenkinses. Peter was a retiring but very knowledgeable man, utterly dedicated to his work, and I always felt that he was the best Park Warden in Kenya. Sarah was charming. They had two small children, a boy and a girl, and they could not have been more friendly or hospitable. Their house was very attractive, with big acacias in front and a stream some sixty yards away where elephant, rhino, buffalo and antelope often came down to drink while we were sitting on the verandah. Fish-eagles in the trees gave their distinctive cries throughout the day and lion roared close to the house at night. Peter and Sarah had two serval cats which they had brought up since they were tiny kittens with their eyes barely open. Now the cats were fully grown; fascinating and beautiful, they stood about eighteen inches high. They were never shut up, night or day, and were devoted to Mark, the Jenkinses' small son. They went for walks with him like a couple of dogs and came when he called them. At night they slept curled up on his bed, but often slipped out through the open bedroom window before dawn. I have increasingly found over the years that I am more interested to see such animals as serval cats, civets, genets and mongooses than lion, elephant, buffalo or even rhino.

Meru National Park was largely covered with bush and the ground was stony, which had the advantage of making it generally difficult for a car to get off the roads. A stretch of the Tana River formed the southern boundary of the park. Two clear, fast streams, the Ura and Rojewero, flowed down through the park into the Tana. While I was on patrol I carried a rifle and a pack on my back like the seven Game Rangers who accompanied me. Every so often Peter would meet us in his Land Rover at a pre-arranged spot to hear our news and bring us some more rations. We moved about throughout the day, and in the evening selected somewhere to spend the night. Whenever we saw elephant, buffalo or lion, which we did frequently, the Game Rangers paid little heed to them except to keep downwind; but if somebody called out, 'Faro!', the Swahili word for rhinoceros, I noticed that everyone immediately looked for a convenient tree. More than once a rhino did charge upwind towards us.

Peter had asked us to destroy any beehives which we found hung up in trees, since their presence gave the owners an excuse to come into the park and poach. We found several of these hives. Kibo would then climb up a tree and cut the hive loose so that it fell to the ground below. He showed no fear of the bees which swarmed round him in the tree but apparently never stung him. I kept some distance away with Erope and Lowassa, but did get stung several times.

Later Peter sent me to investigate an area adjacent to the park on its eastern boundary, where nobody had been for some years and which he felt convinced was heavily poached and harboured poachers who entered the park from there. We searched the area thoroughly for a week but failed to find anybody there. The poachers had probably got word of our presence.

I had met Bill Woodley, the park Warden of Mount Kenya and the Aberdares, before I went to Meru and told him that I was anxious to go up Mount Kenya. I explained to him that although I had travelled extensively in the Karakorams and the Hindu Kush, I was not a mountaineer, having only been on a rope once in my life. I had been up Kilimanjaro and now wanted to see Mount Kenya, the second-highest mountain in Africa. When I asked for his advice, Bill suggested I should spend a day walking right round the top of the mountain and volunteered to find me an efficient guide. He had the guide, a middle-aged, active man, waiting for me when I went to his headquarters in the Aberdares in February 1971. Bill said, 'He knows every corner of the mountain. When he was with Mau Mau, I spent weeks trying to capture him.' The man grinned and said, 'Yes, but though you tried very hard, you never did catch me!' They reminded me of two men who had played football for different schools and were now reminiscing about a famous match in which they had both played. During the thirty years I have lived in Kenya, I have never encountered resentment of Europeans or latent hostility towards them as a result of Mau Mau. I attribute this to Jomo Kenyatta's insistence when he became President that the past must be forgotten and forgiven and everybody in the country must work together to build a new independent Kenya. Fortunately, those Europeans who felt unable to accept this left the country and the remainder have identified themselves with the Kenya of today.

With Erope, Lowassa and Kibo I motored through the rainforest by the Naro Moru park entrance to the bottom of the so-called 'vertical bog', an area of steep mountain bog, where we left the car. Then, with two porters we had collected at Naro Moru and accompanied by our guide, we laboured across the 'vertical bog' and then walked up among the giant groundsel and lobelias, vegetation unique to African mountains, to Two Tarn Hut which Bill Woodley had reserved for us. I had been fortunate enough to have known Eric Shipton who, in 1929 with two companions, was the first to climb Mount Kenya's twin peaks, Nelion (17,022 feet) and Batian (17,058 feet), since Sir Halford Mackinder's pioneering ascent thirty years before. Having read and been moved by Shipton's book, *Upon that Mountain*, I was determined to meet him and by doing so met a truly outstanding man. Though I knew he was a magnificent mountaineer, I always felt that Shipton had been primarily a mountain-explorer, anxious to discover what lay on the far side of a mountain rather than to have conquered its steepest face.

Lowassa had started to cough and I felt anxious about him, knowing how often people developed high-altitude pulmonary oedema, a severe congestion of the lungs, on this mountain. This can be fatal unless the victim is promptly taken down to a lower altitude. As yet, Lowassa showed no symptoms; even so I decided that next day he must rest quietly in the hut, while with Erope, Kibo and the guide I made our circuit of the mountain. This disappointed Lowassa and he protested, but I insisted that he should remain behind with the porters.

We were on snow before we reached Lenana, the third-highest point on Mount Kenya, and on ice before we reached its summit. We went cautiously, having neither crampons, nor an ice-axe with which to cut steps. Fortunately, it was a clear day and there was a spectacular view all round from the summit. Though we had put on our warmest clothes, at this altitude, 16,355 feet, it was bitterly cold and so we did not linger.

It was hard-going once we were off Lenana. We kept as high as we could but we had to cross a succession of steep valleys running down the mountain, their sides covered with loose scree. Immediately above us towered the sheer-sided, snow-capped peaks of Nelion and Batian, riven with gorges, and below an expanse of lesser mountains and desert country extending indefinitely to the north. We passed the wreck of a helicopter which had crashed when attempting to rescue some injured mountaineers. Here there was no other evidence of human activity. For me, this mountain with its fascinating variety of peaks, glaciers and gorges was more exciting than Kilimanjaro which was at its best when seen from a distance.

Lowassa was all right when we got back to Two Tarn Hut, nine hours after leaving it, and we went down the mountain again the following day. I felt a personal sense of achievement having circuited Mount Kenya in a single day.

Lowassa and Kibo went back to their families when we returned from the mountain to Maralal, and shortly after this I flew back to London.

For some time past I had taken my mother abroad each year for a month or so. Among other countries, we had been to Palestine, Italy, Spain and Portugal. In 1969 we returned to Morocco and visited the cities we had seen before and then penetrated south of the Anti-Atlas, a remarkable feat considering that my mother was eighty-nine at the time. Now we went back for a month's visit to Portugal. She was ninety-one and getting frail; she could by then hardly recognize anybody or remember anything. Two years earlier in Morocco her memory had been surprisingly good.

When I returned to Kenya in early July, Erope and Lowassa rejoined me and with them a very intelligent and likeable young Samburu called Kisau. The four of us motored to Mount Elgon and there we climbed up through the forest to the dark, extensive caves. Inside, the countless bats made a subdued but persistent sound. Elephant enter these caves and with their tusks break lumps off the walls for the minerals which this earth contains. From the caves we continued on up to the summit, across which runs the boundary with Uganda.

Later I revisited the Maasai Mara Reserve where Denis Zaphiro and I had had the place to ourselves in 1968; but now I was upset by the increase in the number of lodges, camps and tourist cars. Today, tourists pay large sums to fly over the park and photograph the animals from hot-air balloons; their presence looming overhead unquestionably disturbs the animals. For me the introduction of balloons to the Maasai Mara is the final desecration and I have no desire ever to go back there.

The following year, Rodney Elliott told me that Lord Airlie and Lord Hambleden were proposing to do a camel safari up the east side of the Mathews Range, starting from Lodosoit. I had known Lord Airlie's father when I was an Honorary Attaché to the Duke of Gloucester's mission to Haile Selassie's coronation at Addis Ababa. Lord Airlie's father had then been Comptroller to the Duke. I was only just twenty at the time, and he had been kind and helpful to me in this unfamiliar company and setting. I was now anxious to meet his son.

On my way to Lodosoit I encountered a party of Game Rangers who were to join the Airlie safari. The previous night when the Game Rangers had been camping on their way to Lodosoit, a lion had picked up one of them in his blanket and carried him off. His shouts had aroused the others and the lion had dropped him, unharmed, still rolled in his blanket. He showed me a slight scratch on one arm, the only wound he had sustained as a result of this terrifying experience. Presumably the lion had intended to carry him off and eat him.

René Babault was the hunter in charge of the party and his assistant had failed him at the last moment. He suggested that I should come along with him and act as his second hunter. He lent me a heavy rifle so that, if necessary, I could protect David Airlie's son and Hambleden's three boys while they were shooting birds. I suggested that Erope should be allowed to join them with my shotgun. This he did over the ensuing ten days and he got on very well with them. According to David's description, the five of them led by Erope apparently chased guinea fowl until they eventually took cover under bushes, then flushed the birds and shot them.

I had never been on a safari like this before. There were forty camels and twelve horses for Airlie, his son David, Hambleden and his Italian wife, three boys and a girl. I enjoyed the novelty of this extraordinary safari and the company of the Airlies, the Hambledens and René Babault. We crossed the Milgis and continued up the east side of the Ndotos to Ngoronet. The first few days had been hot but after that we camped beside various streams, the last of which near Ngoronet had a refreshingly cold pool which was large enough to swim in. I was sorry to part with them at Ngoronet and hoped to see more of René Babault. Tragically, he was killed some time later when a light aeroplane in which he was travelling crashed on take-off.

Ever since I was six or seven years old I was determined to shoot big game. I achieved this in 1930 when I hunted African big game for a month in the Danakil country on my own. I was then twenty years old, and tried without success to shoot a buffalo. I hunted big game during my nine-month exploration of the Awash River in 1933–34. And then, taking every opportunity when I was an Assistant DC, I hunted in Northern Darfur and the Upper Nile Province of the Sudan. I learned to hunt, and did all my hunting on my own in remote areas and continued to do so until I no longer wished to hunt. I shall always be thankful that I did not start hunting under the supervision of a white hunter in Kenya, travelling in cars and restricted to hunting in a specific shooting block in the Hemingway manner. I do, however, question whether it has been advantageous to forbid all hunting in Kenya, since now the country is no longer patrolled by hunting parties who can report on poaching. Hunting was big business in Kenya which, thank God, it was not in the Sudan. In the Sudan, provided you took out a General Licence, which specified the permitted species and numbers which could be shot, you were entitled to hunt anywhere without any supervision. When I went there 'Pongo' Barker had succeeded Capt. H.C. Brocklehurst who for years had been the dedicated and outstanding Game Warden in the Sudan. 'Pongo' Barker spent his time looking after the Khartoum Zoo and playing bridge. At that time there was no other Game Warden in the Sudan. In five years I shot seventy lion and one leopard and I was charged by lion sixteen times, often at close quarters; once a charging lion knocked me down. By shooting these lion I saved a number of lives. In Northern Darfur, the Bani Husain and the Zaghawa tribes, among others, regarded it as a matter of honour to hunt down and kill a lion if it had killed any of their animals; cows, camels or horses. In Kutum district, unlike the southern Sudan, there was very little natural prey for lion which lived largely off the tribesmen's herds. The Bani Husain rode down a lion on their horses and bayed it before closing in on it on foot and killing it with their long-bladed spears. I joined them in riding down the lion, but used a rifle instead of a spear to kill it. None of these tribes carries shields, as do the Maasai, when spearing lion. Almost inevitably one or more were killed on each occasion and several mauled.

Once I was fetched to a village a considerable distance away where a lion had just killed a cow. I got a fleeting opportunity to shoot it, but missed. The next time it killed a cow the villagers went after it themselves and suffered seven casualties, four of them fatal.

It was a curious fact that no DC had previously shot a lion in Kutum District. On my arrival in Khartoum, when I spoke to 'Pongo' Barker, he enumerated the most interesting animals to hunt in the district I was going to – addax, white oryx and Barbary sheep – but did not mention lion. I asked him if there were any and he said, 'Yes, there are, but you won't get one. No one has ever shot one there yet.' I was determined I would and I shot thirty there and forty more in the Upper Nile. Lion and leopard were so numerous, they were regarded as vermin at that time in the Sudan and no licence was required to shoot either of them. I shot three lion on my first day, one the day after and another on the third day; this one knocked me down and mauled three of my companions.

I never shot a lion over a bait or at night or used a car when hunting. Our cars were the only two in the district and of course there were none in the Upper Nile swamps. Increasingly, I felt that I would eventually be killed by a lion, but felt the same urge to go on hunting them that a Grand National jockey must feel who rides continually in this race. When I was hunting for sport, for instance, mountain nyala, addax or Barbary sheep, my object was to shoot a really good head if possible and once I had got that I had no desire to shoot another; consequently I shot selectively and seldom except when I had to feed my porters in the southern Sudan.

While I was in the Marshes of southern Iraq I shot a large number of wild boar, which abounded there and were dangerous and destructive; but since then in Kenya I have only shot an occasional animal for meat. I no longer have the desire to shoot, but I do not for a moment regret the years I have spent hunting which gave me some of the most exciting moments in my life. In Kenya I had become tired of seeing endless lion from cars in game parks, sometimes as many as twenty or thirty in a morning. Seeing them like this robbed them of all individuality, and indeed became a bore. This was never the case when hunting lion on foot in the Sudan, or occasionally encountering them while I travelled on foot in the NFD.

While I was in India in 1983 and 1984, I twice visited the

Bandhavgarh tiger sanctuary in Bhopal and stayed in what had previously been the Maharaja of Rewa's hunting lodge. There were only six bedrooms so that it could not accommodate many visitors. The first time I stayed there for a week and went out each morning before sunrise on one of the lodge's six elephant. I went back to Bandhavgarh with Pamela, Lady Egremont, who had previously never seen a tiger. We saw a very large leopard, a herd of gaur, and seven tigers in four days. Each day I saw tigers, sometimes a tiger was on a kill. The mahout would stop the elephant within ten feet of a tiger. The tiger showed complete indifference towards it, but if the elephant came yet a little closer, the tiger might look up and snarl and the mahout would edge it back. I was fascinated by these magnificent beasts. To me, tigers, with their splendid colouring, are much more impressive than lion. Once we were able to trace a tigress's movements through the jungle by the alarm calls made by langur, sambhar and chital, as she approached us; and we heard her cubs greet her on a small cliff nearby.

I was always fascinated watching and hearing how the mahout controlled his elephant with his *ankus*, a touch of his toe or a few muttered words; stopping it, moving it to right or left, or telling it to lift or push down a branch that barred our progress. Moving noiselessly through the jungle on an elephant, I had felt associated with my surroundings. I could never have shot another elephant after this intimate association with them.

Baragoi was on the road to the north and I motored through there every now and again, partly to find out for Rodney Elliott about the movement of poachers in the area between there and Marsabit. There was a small primary school at Baragoi and most of the boys in it were aged between seven and twelve. On my way through Baragoi I used to stop my car under some trees near the school and the boys would come over and ask if they could play boxing. At Erope's insistence I had bought two pairs of gloves and we carried these in the car. One small boy in particular caught my attention and he invariably came over to greet me whenever I stopped near the school. Once, when I looked about for him, I couldn't see him anywhere. Feeling anxious in case something had happened to him, I went over and asked one of the children, 'Where is Lawi?' The boy replied, 'He's in your car.' I went back to it and found Lawi sitting in the front seat. I said, 'What are you doing in the car, Lawi?', to which he replied, 'I don't know. I'm leaving school and I'm going to stay with you,' and so we drove off together. This was in 1972, and Lawi was perhaps eleven or twelve years old at the time; he has now been with me for over twenty years. His parents were in Maralal and seemed quite happy that he should join me. He had until then been living at Ololokwe with his grandmother, to whom he was devoted.

In 1988 Lawi was elected a member of the Maralal Urban Council and the Council elected him their chairman. Consequently he was known as the mayor. He acted in Harry Hook's film, *The Kitchen Toto*, in my opinion the best feature film to come out of Africa. Lawi played the part of the corporal who picks the dead kitchen-boy out of the river.

In 1973 Peter Jenkins was starting a game reserve, to be called Sibiloi, at the north-east end of Lake Turkana. It would include Koobi Fora where for some time Richard Leakey had been excavating the fossil remains of prehistoric man. Peter asked me to assist him and we went up there together to inspect the area. Too occupied elsewhere to spend longer at Sibiloi, he left me on my own in charge of the camp for two months.

The new reserve was adjacent to Merille country, just across the Ethiopian frontier, and in consequence in an area frequently raided by these formidable tribesmen. I had six Game Rangers, one of them a Turkana sergeant; Erope and Kisau were with me and I had borrowed a rifle from the Game Department together with sufficient ammunition in case we were attacked. I always felt it was possible the Merille might attack us at night in order to acquire our rifles. I had been as far as Alia Bay during my 1969 journey, but had not seen this country to the north of it. Much of it was thorn bush; I generally travelled in my Land Rover with two or more Game Rangers as well as Erope. We were travelling along when we came across the corpse of a naked youth on the track, who had been speared. He had a curious wound on the surface of his stomach where his navel had recently been removed. When I questioned one of the Rangers about this, he said, 'Don't you know the Merille always cut out the navel from anybody they have killed?' I thought this was a strange method of mutilation and one I had never heard of before, though during my long journey through the Danakil country in 1933–34, I had become well aware that the Danakil invariably castrated anyone they had killed or wounded as proof. This to me seemed a more rational method of mutilation than excising someone's navel.

As we motored on, one of the Rangers noticed a man hiding in a nearby luggah. We stopped and picked him up. He had managed to escape when some Merille surprised him and killed his companion and he was now very wrought-up. We took him back to camp. I warned our sentries once again to be especially alert at night. The Turkana sergeant, whom I disliked, tended to spend his time in bed instead of supervising the sentries he had posted. I now insisted forcibly on his doing so, and at intervals during the night checked the sentries myself. Shortly after this I took the opportunity to send the sergeant back to Peter at Marsabit and he sent me a replacement. The Sibiloi park still exists today, but, owing to its remoteness, it is seldom visited; however, its very remoteness and the number of animals to be found there make travelling there a rewarding experience.

In November 1973 I returned to Maralal and after a few days went on to Nairobi. As I got out of the car at John Seago's house, John said to me, 'So, you got my telegram?' I said, 'No, I left Maralal a week ago.' He told me that my mother had died three days before, very peacefully in her sleep. I said, 'Thank God for that.'

When I was last in London, time and again she had repeated, 'I just wish that I could die quietly . . . I just wish that I could die quietly.' Now that this had finally happened I could only feel thankful. She had not been in any pain, but her mind had gone completely and in a way I think she had been conscious of this. Such a tragic, lingering end to a life that had meant so much to many, and especially to me, had distressed me enormously. We had always meant so much to each other.

A year later, Kisau died of hepatitis B. Ever since we had been together he had taken every opportunity to help me and I had been rewarding him by teaching him to drive on our way to Baragoi. There he developed the symptoms and I took him to see the Catholic Mission sister in the clinic. She told me to take him at once to the hospital in Wamba. During the examination, the doctor looked up at me and shook his head; Kisau died two days later. Since 1930 I had spent my time travelling in remote and often dangerous areas where any of my companions might have been killed or have died from one cause or another. Yet, after all these years, this was the first time one of them had died. Kisau had only been with me for a short time. He had been such a happy, cheerful and enterprising lad and he seemed to have identified himself completely with me. His sudden and unexpected death shook me badly.

CHAPTER NINE

Samburu Initiations

BY NOW I NO LONGER used camels for my journeys. I had used camels when they were the obvious method of travelling in the NFD and still did so on anti-poaching patrols. I still much preferred travelling with camels but now it would have been ridiculous to do so when I could equally well use a Land Rover.

More and more I found myself based on Maralal, camping at a variety of sites on the outskirts of the town. Erope and Lawi were permanently with me. Erope was a Turkana from Lodwar, whereas Lawi was a Samburu whose *manyatta* was close to Maralal. Increasingly I found myself involved with Lawi's family.

In July 1976, initiation ceremonies marking a new Samburu age-set began. These ceremonies took place on average every fourteen years and began after the Lmasula clan had killed a bull on Mount Nyiru, the sacred mountain. Lawi, who belonged to the Lkuwono, or blacksmith's clan, always the first clan to be initiated, was now old enough to be circumcised. On my journey with Frank Steele in 1960, I had seen groups of boys wandering about in the black cloaks which they wore for some time before and after they had been circumcised; they were the 1960 age-set. But as yet I had seen none of the ceremonies themselves. Now I was so closely involved with Lawi's family that as one of them I witnessed not only the circumcisions of the initiates but the ceremonies which went with them.

Like all the other clans, the Lkuwono selected a site for their *lorora* or circumcision camp. Each *lorora* was situated if possible near woodland where there was also sufficient water and grazing. The *lorora* comprised an extensive area enclosed by a thorn fence inside which the women of each family built a windowless, flat-roofed hut made of sticks and branches. These huts were covered with grass and the walls and roof plastered with cow-dung; a hole in the roof let out the ever-present smoke. There was an enclosure for their cattle and each hut stood adjacent to the next, sited round the perimeter of the fence according to the family's lineage. Each family had a separate gateway for its cattle. At the centre of the *lorora* was a fire where the elders gathered in the evenings and talked, argued incessantly, and prayed to the Samburu god, Nkai. This fire was not allowed to die out.

Perhaps two months before his circumcision, Lawi put on his goatskin cape made of three skins dyed black with charcoal mixed with animal fat. Then, with a group of boys, he went off to gather a suitable stick to make the shaft of his bow from one place, sticks for his arrows from another and gum, with which to blunt the points of eight arrows, from yet a third place. Each of these was collected from certain traditional areas, often far apart, such as South Horr, Baringo and Marsabit. The initiates might be gone for a week or more, particularly when collecting gum.

The day before their circumcision, all the boys in the *lorora* went off at a run, each carrying a gourd to fetch water from a traditional permanent spring – in Lawi's case to Kisima, a distance of at least twenty-four miles there and back from his *lorora*. Before their circumcision the boys wore their hair in a circular tuft; but now, on their return with the water, their mothers shaved their heads and two men who were the sponsors for each boy made him a pair of sandals from the skin of an ox that had been killed the day before. A few families circumcised their boys that evening, all the others the following morning. Throughout the night the initiates sang the *lebarta*, the circumcision song. This mass singing was immensely moving and impressive in the dark. There were only a few men in the area who knew how to circumcise. Some were really competent at performing this peculiar and intricate form of Samburu operation, others were less so.

The boys to be circumcised might number as many as two hundred in a *lorora*, and the circumcisions began almost before it got light. Any man or boy could watch, but no woman was allowed near. The boy, who was naked, sat on a fresh ox-skin, leaning back against one of his sponsors, who held his shoulders, while the other sponsor held his right leg; another man, usually a close relative, held his left leg. That year I saw many boys being circumcised; they remained absolutely motionless throughout the operation, barely blinking. They would have been permanently disgraced if they had shown the slightest sign of pain. If a boy had flinched, his family's cattle would have been driven out of the *lorora*, smashing through the perimeter fence; then cow-dung and, on top of this, hot ash would have been rubbed in his mother's hair. After a boy's circumcision, a man beat his right thigh twice and said, 'Stand up, you are now a man.' Before standing up, the boy would sing a *lebarta* asking for an ox from his family. The ox was shot in its jugular vein with a blocked arrow and the boy drank its fresh blood mixed in milk. The arrow wound was then smeared with dung and the ox was sent off to graze. For two weeks the boys were not allowed to drink water and were given meat, blood and milk for food. They were not allowed to wash in water until the ceremony of the arrows a month later.

The day after circumcision, the boys' sponsors fashioned their bows and arrows and in nearly every case fastened a black ostrich feather on either side of the boys' heads. A day or two later, using four of the eight blunted arrows, they started shooting small birds, skinned each one, stuffed it with grass and hung it down from the back of their head. They were also entitled to chase and shoot at uncircumcised girls as they ran away from them, aiming at their ankles, unless the girls ransomed themselves with beads. A senior Samburu official standing beside me on one occasion said, 'You will never realize how important all this is to us. It is the most important event in our lives.'

Perhaps a month later, there followed the ceremony of *Lmuget Loolbaa*, the casting away of the arrows; after this ceremony, the initiate became a *moran*. All the families killed and roasted an ox over an open fire. Each boy then attempted to break the ox's hip-bone with one blow of a club. He then took a piece of the roasted rump, stuck on a knifeblade, gave it to his mother and said to her, 'Mother, this is the food I was eating when I was young. I am returning it to you. Never give me food again.' They gave the traditional strings of beads they had worn to their mothers and were rubbed all over with red ochre. From now on, as long as they were *moran* they might never eat in the presence of women, indeed anywhere where women were in sight. These ceremonies involved the slaughter by the family of a succession of sheep and oxen. At the conclusion of the ceremonies, the Lmasula clan killed another bull on Mount Nyiru.

I am exasperated when European women intrude into tribal ceremonies which exclude women, presumably because they consider that, being Europeans, tribal restrictions do not apply to them. During one of the initiation ceremonies which I have just described, an Englishwoman was present at the circumcisions. I resented this and said so. On another occasion, the throwing away of the arrows, when some sixty initiates were sitting on a bank waiting to be feasted on the meat which had been killed for them, two Englishwomen went and sat beside them. On yet another occasion when only a few boys were being circumcised, a car appeared as it got light with four Italians in it, two girls and two men. The chief asked me to tell them that, while any man could be present at the circumcisions, women were prohibited from doing so. I went over and told them and the car went off some distance with the girls. The two men came to watch. As the first boy was being circumcised, one of the Italians fainted and fell into the thorn fence beside him.

Nigel Pavitt in his book *Samburu* has written a definitive account of this tribe. Previously, the only two books on the tribe were by Paul Spencer, an anthropologist, and I must confess that I find both Spencer's books too technical to make easy reading. I was told by the British DC that during his time with the Samburu, Spencer dressed as a *moran* and on one occasion came into his office and besought him to mediate in a case in which his 'cousins' were involved. In view of this close relationship with a Samburu family which he was attempting to acquire, it was unfortunate that, having spent three years studying the Samburu, Spencer had to leave Kenya in order to write up his thesis the year before these all-important initiation ceremonies took place. In contrast to Nigel Pavitt's detailed account, they are only scantily dealt with in Spencer's book and then only by hearsay.

Nigel's book is splendidly illustrated with his own colour photographs, every one of which is relevant to the text, and it deals with every aspect of Samburu life. He lives in Nairobi and I always look forward immensely to his visits, which are all too infrequent.

Soon after these ceremonies were finally over, in January 1977, I went to San'a in North Yemen and stayed with Hugh Leach. I then went on to Muscat, Salalah, Nazwa and Ibri in Oman and met up again with bin Kabina and bin Ghabaisha, who had been my constant companions during the years I spent travelling with the Rashid. From Abu Dhabi I returned to London, and in July flew to Delhi and from there to Singapore and on to Bali. There I joined Gavin Young on a 42-foot ketch, *Fiona*, which he had chartered with its owner Brian MacGarry, known to us as 'Mac', on board. We sailed through the Lombok straits to Kalimantan (Borneo) and north up the coast to the Kelai River, the Celebes Sea and across to Brunei, Sarawak, and Singapore.

This had been a fascinating experience. For me the challenge of the sea had always had a rather distant appeal. During long vacations at Oxford I had worked my passage to Istanbul for two months on a tramp steamer and after that for a month on a trawler fishing off Iceland. I had also sailed for a fortnight on a dhow in the Persian Gulf. But on *Fiona* with only three of us on board I was really close to the sea in an exotic tropical setting. Gavin was the best of company in contrast to Mac, *Fiona*'s owner, whose language was one long obscenity. This is always tiresome. Gavin had sailed to Singapore from Brunei on the *Rajah Brooke* and left the two of us to take *Fiona* to Singapore.

Fiona's engine had packed up before we reached Brunei. There had been a hurricane before we set out and the sea was still running high. Mac had mentioned ten-foot waves. One night, as we approached Singapore, I was on watch, and very early I thought I saw an island ahead of us. I shouted down to Mac who came on deck. By now we could make out a line of reefs in the distance to the south with the surf breaking high into the air.

Mac checked our position on his chart and said, 'Thank God, we're just where we should be. Go down and get some sleep. I'll call you as soon as we're round that point and then we'll have some breakfast.' A couple of hours later Mac woke me with a flood of obscenities as he came down the companion-way. I said, 'Christ, what's the matter now, Mac?' He replied, 'The only thing that's certain is fucking death!', a nice way to be woken up in the morning. He went on, 'The wind has failed completely and we're drifting on to the reefs.' From the deck I could see that they were much closer. I asked him how long *Fiona* would last when we struck them. He said, 'She'll be gone in two minutes.' From time to time, the wind would get up, only to die away all too soon. It took us eight hours to get round the point which Mac had hoped to weather in time for breakfast. By then the reefs were very close.

From Singapore, where we left the boat, I visited Malaysia, Delhi and Hyderabad before returning to England in April.

I met Sir Robert ffolkes for the first time in Delhi in January 1978, while he was working with the Save the Children Fund in Ladakh. He suggested I should visit him there, which I did during September and October 1983. I had always regretted that I never saw Tibet before the Chinese invasion. I have no wish to see it now. However, Ladakh's culture is Buddhist and Tibetan and while I was with Sir Robert there I lived with a people who were akin to them and met refugee Tibetans. For two months we travelled with ponies and sometimes yaks from one traditional and as yet unchanged village to the next. As Sir Robert's companion I was welcomed by the villagers in their houses and this gave me the opportunity to take some splendid portraits of these fascinating, timeless people, the like of whom I had never seen before.

I continue to meet adventurous young men who wish they could lead the life I have led. I was only just in time to do so myself. Now, in a fast-changing world, it is too late. Perhaps something might be found of an unspoilt past in northern China; had I been a few years younger I might have gone there to satisfy myself that this was so.

In June 1978 I flew back to Kenya. Before leaving in 1977 I had got Lawi a job with Myles Burton's safari firm; Myles had taken him on sight. I had given Erope my tent and enough money to buy some animals, since I was thinking of perhaps staying on indefinitely with a tribal people in India after I left the Yemen. The day after I got back to Nairobi I ran into Lawi driving one of Myles Burton's safari lorries past John Seago's house. He jumped out of the lorry, came over, embraced me and called out to his co-driver, 'Take this lorry back to Myles and tell him I've left him and rejoined my father.' I asked him where Erope was. He said, 'I don't know. The last time I saw him he told me that somehow he was going to get hold of a rifle and join the Nyoroko. I've had no news of him since then.'

I heard recently that Erope had been killed on the Sudan border. He had become one of the leaders of the formidable and notorious Nyoroko outlaws. Later he was involved with the Toposa tribe in the chaotic fighting that was going on in the southern Sudan. Once when I was dining at Magdalen and was talking about Kenya, I mentioned what had happened to Erope after he left me. Someone said, 'Surely you can't approve of what he's done?' I replied, 'It's just what I'd probably have done if I'd been Erope. After all, he typifies the Kenyan version of Rob Roy.'

Erope could neither read nor write; I had tried to teach him the alphabet, but he couldn't be bothered with it and consequently was illiterate. In his spare time, he became a prosperous merchant and sold cattle meat to the Sudanese Army. Aged thirty-five, he was killed by hostile tribesmen raiding his cattle. I had been very fond of him and had always been hoping to meet him again.

Myles Burton understandably thought that Lawi had treated him rather badly, but I felt that nothing had mattered to Lawi except being back with me. We drove back to Maralal from Nairobi and a day or two later Lawi said to me, 'Why do we go on living like this in tents, *mzee juu*?' – *mzee juu*, 'top elder', had been my nickname over the years – 'Why don't you build a house?' I said to him, 'I own no land here, so how can I build a house?' and he replied, 'I can put one anywhere I like.' We were camped in a valley a mile or so east of the town with a hill immediately above us. The next morning, we walked up this hill and chose a site for the house under some wild olives with a spacious view. The day after, with the help of Lawi's father, we started to build the house. At that time we could see some Samburu *manyattas*, but nowhere any tin roofs which now unfortunately are becoming commonplace. When I had come here in 1961 all the country below us had been forest. Now, except for an occasional tree, this forest has all been cut down or burnt. For some years we were able to use the treestumps for firewood.

We levelled a small patch of ground under some of the trees and dug a shallow trench outlining the house. In the trench, we set up nine-foot-high cedar poles adjacent to each other, for the outer wall, and divided the house into three rectangular rooms of roughly equal size, ten feet by twelve, each with a window but with only one outer door in the central room. We obtained the roof timbers from Siddiq Bhola, and employed a local builder to put on a pitched roof of corrugated iron which was admittedly unsightly but conveniently weathertight. We concreted the floor and plastered the inside walls with a mixture of mud and cow-dung. We then bought some basic furniture in the town and put up a shelter outside the house for the kitchen, where we cooked on three stones. We also fastened gutters to the roof to catch water in drums when it rained. We built a verandah in front of the house and after that started to plant a garden. Today this garden is very colourful; the bougainvilleas especially are magnificent.

Soon after we had finished the house, Gavin Young came out and stayed with us for a fortnight; unfortunately this was as much time as he could spare. As I had expected he enjoyed this life and was as popular here as he had been among the Marshmen of southern Iraq.

Before independence, when I first came to Kenya, Maralal had been the Samburu district headquarters and it has remained as such. At first I regarded it as little more than a stopping-off point, but after Lawi and I had built this house Maralal inevitably became our base. By then John Seago had died. I had become very attached to him but sadly had seen less and less of him because I lived almost entirely up north. A small, rather frail-looking man, he had suffered from tuberculosis. During the war, in 1940, he had gone to sea and despite his ill-health had been given command of an armed trawler, crewed largely by his friends, which patrolled the English coast. This he continued to do throughout the war. After the war, for health reasons, he was advised to live in East Africa. He came to Kenya and became increasingly involved with wildlife, in which he had long been interested. Tony Parkinson, John's godson and business partner, had grown up in Norfolk. Both of them were absorbed with the countryside and its wildlife. When John came to Kenya he took Tony with him and for twenty-six years they worked together trapping animals. Tony Parkinson was an all-rounder, a good driver, mechanic, boxer and tennis player. Eventually, John let Tony have his family home in Essex, where John had previously established Tony's father and mother. Soon after this, Tony went to the Philippines where he married a Filipina. Now, to John's distress, Tony did not see him again, although he continued to write to John to urge him to join them in the Philippines.

For some years after I first arrived in Kenya, I had met none of the ranchers who lived in the White Highlands. One day I encountered Mike and Jane Prettejohn who were camping at Baragoi and they invited me to come and stay with them. Mike had been a white hunter. Rodney Elliott had described him to me as at that time one of the very best in Kenya. A rather silent man, some people dismissed him as dull; sharing, as I did, many of his interests, I certainly never found this to be the case. His wife Jane had previously been married to Hilary Hook. She was a delightful and very attractive woman. Both of them became close friends of mine. I always enjoyed staying on their ranch on the plain below the Aberdares Country Club at Mweiga. They lived in a sunny, single-storey house with a long, open verandah from which, beyond the garden, there was a fine view of Mount Kenya. There were elephant, buffalo and a variety of other animals on the ranch.

Meeting the Prettejohns had been a breakthrough for me. Until then I had confined my interest to what had previously been the Northern Frontier District, its tribes and the administrative officials and Game Wardens whom I encountered there, with little or any desire to meet the European settlers living in the White Highlands. Indeed, I had been resentful of their presence, their fences and farms. The exception was Anne Joyce, whom I had first met when she was a girl of sixteen and was visiting her grandmother who lived near us in Wales. I met her again soon after my arrival in Kenya. She had inherited from her father a large ranch in the Wakamba country on the border of the Maasai country, near Machakos. Typically, at the end of her life when she eventually left her ranch to live in Nairobi, she refused offers from the Europeans who wished to buy it and insisted that it was acquired by the Wakamba who had worked for her. Anne was in every sense a great lady and I have heard her reliably described by an American authority as one of the most outstanding ranchers in the world. I liked her enormously. Through the Prettejohns I met Sandy Field and also Bill Harris at Nanyuki. Bill Harris, a regular soldier, had served under Wingate during his campaign in Gojjam commanding a company of the Sudan Defence Force. We were together in the same battle when he was wounded. Throughout this campaign I was fighting with the Ethiopian Patriots instead of serving with the Sudan Defence Force. Bill always claims that I came out of the bush one morning and ate the whole of his last pot of marmalade for breakfast, saying as I did so, 'By Jove, that's good. Of course, it's easy for you to get another pot!' He is fond of telling this story and I have heard it repeated by a number of people. Thirty years later, when I met Bill again in Kenya for the first time since the war, I walked into his room, came to attention, put a pot of marmalade on the table behind which he was sitting, and said, 'Repaid.'

Streets in Maralal

Lawi's house as we first built it

His new house built alongside the old one

Lawi after his circumcision in 1976

Lawi as the mayor of Maralal

Laputa in 1981

Namitu and her baby daughter

Above Laputa's house

Left Sandy and Bushboy, with Talone in front, on the steps of Laputa's house

Right Kibiriti with his children
Below Lopego

Faces of Kenya: a Samburu *moran* at Wamba (*opposite*); a Turkana woman (*above left*); a Samburu dressed in his black circumcision cloak (*above right*); a Pokot at Amaya (*below left*); a Samburu woman (*below right*)

Leopard with its kill

Vultures and hyenas on a lion kill

Ahmed, the famous Marsabit elephant, photographed by Peter Jenkins

Below The escarpment at Malossa from the 'viewpoint'

Opposite Turkana women preparing for a dance

Overleaf Maasai boy three hours after his circumcision

A Samburu *moran*

Sandy Field had retired from the Colonial Service after serving as a provincial commissioner in Uganda. While he was in Uganda he had been a dedicated elephant hunter and had obtained a magnificent pair of tusks which he kept in a bank in London, going there whenever he was in London to gloat over them. He gave these tusks to the museum at Quex Park in Kent, an estate owned by Christopher Powell-Cotton who, like Sandy Field, had been a provincial commissioner in Uganda. He spoke fluent Turkana which he always used whenever he greeted Kibiriti, one of my retainers. Later, John Owen put Sandy in charge of the Serengeti National Park, which is where I first met him. He then settled down to live in Nanyuki and bought an aeroplane which he used extensively to get about in Kenya. He kept himself well informed about whatever was happening in England, and indeed in the world in general; it was rewarding to stay with him in his meticulous little house in Nanyuki and be brought up to date with world affairs. I was less enthusiastic about flying with him, for he had had two or three narrow escapes. He would 'buzz' the house when he came to Maralal and we would go and fetch him from the nearby landing ground. He was a smallish, quick-moving man, rapid of speech, with an animated expression.

Except for the Catholic missionaries, for many years I have been the only permanent European resident in Maralal. I have always thought of Jasper Evans and Jill, his wife, living on their ranch near Rumuruti sixty miles away, as my nearest white neighbours with whom I keep in touch. Jasper had been in the navy which I should have expected when I met him. The Evanses live in an old-fashioned, two-storey house surrounded by shady trees, bougainvilleas and other flowering shrubs. I always feel immediately at home in this house. Jasper Evans has introduced large numbers of camels into an area where they were previously barely known to exist. Recently he imported twenty-seven fully grown camels from Pakistan to improve the milk yield among his herds. All twenty-seven were somehow or other loaded into a single plane. Recently, I have got to know Nicholas and Heather Day, a delightful couple who live on a ranch about thirty miles away, close enough to go there for lunch, for which they have invited Kibiriti and me on a number of occasions. From time to time Kibiriti has returned their hospitality.

CHAPTER TEN

At Home

I HAVE NEVER DRIVEN a car if I could avoid it, but until I taught Lawi to drive I had no one else to do so. He was a naturally good driver and used to maintain that, whereas I was quite the worst driver in Kenya, I had been a very good instructor. He was remarkably gifted and good at whatever he took up. For instance, when Phil Snyder trained Erope, Lawi, Kibo and myself in mountain-rescue work on some formidable cliffs above the Athi River, Erope hated it and would not go near a precipice. But Phil Snyder said of Lawi, 'He is one of the best natural rock-climbers, European or African, I've ever met.'

When he was twenty-two, Lawi flew to London where he stayed with me for a month in my flat in Chelsea. He had visited Nairobi on a few occasions but had never previously been out of Kenya. From the moment he arrived he seemed completely relaxed in this enormous city. I used to take Lawi, dressed in a dark suit, to lunch at the Travellers' Club. I heard someone we had been lunching with say to him, 'Lawi, you were obviously educated in England. Which school were you at?' We stayed in the country with Tony Rumbold and his wife, with the Oakseys and with the Verneys, and everywhere he seemed at home. We saw the second rehearsal and then Trooping the Colour itself, on both occasions with good seats, and watched the Beating of Retreat. This visit to England had unquestionably given Lawi a perception of a whole new world.

By now Lawi was six feet tall, with very broad shoulders

and narrow hips, an attractive open face, and even in his later teens he had an air of self-possession and quiet authority. When he got married he wore Samburu dress and said to me, 'Anyone who is ashamed of his tribal customs is a slave.'

Now that Erope had left me I was looking for someone else to take his place. One day when Lawi and I were still camped near Maralal, two young Samburu turned up and helped us by fetching wood and making the fire. Lawi said, 'Let's keep that one with us'; but I opted for the other one. I asked him what his name was and he said, 'My father called me Tommy-Gun.' His father had been wounded and lost a leg fighting with the King's African Rifles in the Abyssinian campaign. I said, 'You can't be called that, it's a ridiculous name,' and he replied, 'All right, you give me a name.' I thereupon called him Laputa after the Zulu leader in John Buchan's *Prester John* and since then that has always been his name, even on his identity card and other official papers. A tall, slender figure, he has a rather sombre face with large, expressive, perhaps wistful, eyes.

As I got to know him, I discovered Laputa had a strongly artistic temperament. Some years later when I was living in Lawi's house, I gave Laputa the money to build a house for himself, which he did, on a hillside outside the town from which there was a spacious view across the valley to the Maralal Safari Lodge. It seemed to me that Laputa had selected the most pleasing site in the neighbourhood.

Below the house, the hillside sloped down to a wide shallow valley where water lay after heavy rain; beyond, the intervening ground, covered with acacias, rose gradually to a rim of low forest-covered hills. The slopes opposite the house were frequented by tame zebra, occasionally by eland and a herd of buffalo and sometimes by elephant, especially at night. Fortunately, both the road into the town and the town itself were out of sight, but after dark there was a ring of lights from the small Maralal Safari Lodge and a few houses opposite which were scarcely visible in the daytime. There is still some superb forest near Maralal. The most numerous trees are the junipers, generally called 'pencil cedars', some of them magnificent trees. There had been many on the slopes where Maralal Safari Lodge is situated. Most of these junipers are now dead and the remainder are dying. I first noticed this happening some ten years ago.

At first the very top of the tree dies and this spreads down the tree until just a leafless skeleton remains. It has been suggested to me that this is caused by mites. By now, nearly all the junipers in this neighbourhood are dead and even some of the trees in the forest six miles away to the west of the town are affected. I have a feeling of despair that this blight may eventually destroy the junipers throughout the magnificent forests in Kenya, as has happened to the elms in England. I doubt if anything can be done about it. With the demand for charcoal by an ever-increasing population in Maralal, and since no alternative fuel is available, more and more trees are being cut down to provide it. Neither can I see any solution to this problem.

A year after joining me, Laputa produced Ewoi Ekai, a Turkana of approximately his own age. He had worked for a while in Bhola's garage and was already a capable mechanic. Bhola had nicknamed him Kibiriti, or 'match', by which name he is now almost universally known. He is six feet two inches tall, powerfully built and has aristocratic features marred only by the absence of his four front teeth. He now joined us as a permanent member of our small society. Laputa had spent five years in a primary school and could read and write, whereas

Kibiriti had never been at school and could do neither. Nevertheless, he has been recently elected as the chairman of one of the primary schools in Maralal, a job which he does conscientiously and very efficiently. He has sent his two small sons to this school; they have tried, but to their exasperation failed, to teach their father the alphabet.

I am very fond of Kibiriti who is kind, thoughtful and utterly reliable. His pleasant voice is curiously distinctive and I can pick it up as soon as I hear it. Kibiriti is not only industrious but has a head for business. He is generally popular not only with the Turkana but also with the Samburu. Kibiriti eventually ran a bus, the only public transport between Maralal and Baragoi, but this became uneconomic due to the heavy expense of constantly replacing burst tyres. He has a three-ton lorry which he contracts out, as well as a general store in Baragoi, his home town.

Though he is a Turkana, from a country much too arid for cultivation, Kibiriti has designed and laid out an extensive and attractive garden round his house; this is situated on a flat plain between the hill on which Lawi's house is visible, and the town. A number of poison trees of a uniform shape, a thick, bare trunk crowned by a compact mass of dark-green leaves, are scattered singly on this plain. A deadly poison can be brewed from the roots of this tree, yet elephant and children eat its small, yellow fruit. The Wakamba and Wagiriama among others use this poison with their powerful bows to kill elephant. It is interesting that in a comparatively small area at a very similar altitude, these poison trees are confined to Kibiriti's vicinity.

When Laputa and I had made our garden, Kibiriti, who proved to be a surprisingly knowledgeable, practical gardener, would advise us what to plant and how to prune. Being half-way down a slope there was little soil above the underlying rocks, whereas Kibiriti's garden was planted on richer soil in the valley bottom. We planted bougainvilleas and when these were in flower they attracted sunbirds which are always a delight to watch. Laputa hung a birdtable in one of the trees and flight after flight of starlings, mostly the spectacular Superb starlings, among others, arrived as soon as they saw him going to it in the morning. Weaver birds would be already waiting in the tree. The dawn chorus of birds, as it begins to get light, is varied and unforgettable; and after that comes the sound of approaching cow-bells.

After Lawi got married I moved into Laputa's house. One evening he said to me, 'I want to try and draw.' He told me this was something he had always wanted to do but had never done. I gave him a large sheet of paper and went off to bed while he sat there starting to work by the light of a hurricane lamp. In the morning he showed me a pencil drawing he had made based on photographs of three lion. I was astonished not only by their life-like realism and accurate proportions, but also by the originality with which he had drawn details such as the lion's mane.

Recently an Irish artist, Colin Watson, came out to Kenya to paint my portrait, which now hangs in the Royal Geographical Society. Laputa watched him doing this for some time, then borrowed a brush and oilpaints and did a study on board of a camel's head based on one of my photographs. He had never handled a brush before, yet the result was quite staggering and might have been the work of a professional artist. It hangs in the Yarre Lodge near Maralal for anyone to see. Among other things, Laputa has also produced a pen-and-ink portrait of me which is probably the finest work he has done to date. This portrait has been said to do everything but speak.

Both Laputa's and Kibiriti's houses were built on the same basic pattern as Lawi's, with three adjacent rooms; but whereas Kibiriti's house is on flat ground, Laputa had dug his into the hillside. Overlooking the valley, he had constructed an open verandah with a partially enclosed, roofed area behind it. At one end of the verandah he had another sitting room, its windows enclosed by broad wire-netting and low enough to afford a comfortable view. At the other end of the verandah there was a fully enclosed kitchen. Five concrete steps led down from the verandah to the drive below. The only fuel to be had in Maralal is charcoal and we cook with this over a small brazier called a *jiko*. Water is always a problem and, except during the rains when we catch what rainwater we can off the roof, we never have enough. The British had constructed a dam to supply Maralal and normally we could get water from the town when our water ran out. But in the 1979 drought, the dam dried up and water had to be brought to the town in tankers. We fetched water for ourselves in jerry-cans from twelve miles away. Consequently a bath here was, and always is, a real luxury.

In 1988 Laputa married a Samburu girl called Namitu. Namitu is unusually large, tall and placid, unfailingly cheerful and always eager to help. She is unobtrusively well-educated and speaks good English. She herself keeps the house clean and tidy and, unlike so many of these educated women, is prepared to turn her hand to anything, such as fetching water or wood.

Namitu's father had two wives, each with seven children of whom four were girls. Two of her brothers, who were circumcised in 1990, are now twenty-three and twenty-four years old. Namitu's little brother Ngarientim, whom I christened 'the Bushbaby' when he was perhaps five years old, but who now prefers to be known as 'the Bushboy', is a strongly built and active boy of nine. He has an engaging expression, a gentle, confiding manner and an unusually powerful personality for a boy of his age. He works hard at school and is invariably first in his exams. The two eldest half-brothers by another mother are both *moran*. The elder of these, Sepiri, nicknamed 'Sungura', which means hare, by me, the name by which he is generally known, is just seventeen and is training to become a professional boxer. He is determined to fight for Kenya in the next Olympic Games. He has now been training for seven months with the ABA Club in Nairobi. At present he is a welterweight, thick-set and powerful, but working hard all the time to strengthen his already well-developed muscles. He is very quick on his feet with a stabbing left hand and a knock-out right. He recently fought for the ABA against the Kenya Police and knocked out his opponent in the second round.

Sungura's youngest brother, Talone, a rather delicate-looking boy who is the same age as Ngarientim, copies Sungura. For a child of his age, he has a devastating punch and knows how to use it. Lechiin, Sungura's other brother, is sixteen. He was just old enough to be circumcised with Sungura at the last initiation ceremonies and consequently for a time was known as 'the Mini-Moran'. All three of these brothers have a marked resemblance to one another. I bought Sungura a plot in the town where he has built a shop and two rows of rooms to let; this I hope will bring him in enough money to enable him to go on boxing. Except for Sungura and Namitu's two elder brothers, all those I have mentioned may at any time be sleeping in the house, spread about on the floor of the central room.

My father kept no dogs in the Legation during the years we were in Addis Ababa. When we were at the Milebrook, the first dog I owned was a golden cocker spaniel but it died of distemper after I had had it for a year. I was then ten years old and at prep school. I still remember my grief when I heard the news. I had two other spaniels; the last one I taught to retrieve and I took it everywhere with me, even to Scotland, when I was shooting. When I was stationed at Darfur, no government officials kept dogs. I understood that this was because sometime in the past, when the District Officers had gathered at El Fasher for Christmas, a dog which many of them handled and played with developed rabies. In consequence they had to be evacuated all the way to Khartoum to be inoculated, leaving the province with almost no one to administer it. I never checked this story but the fact remains that officials did not keep dogs. After this, my nomadic life gave me no opportunity to keep a dog until I came to Kenya.

Lawi, Kibriti and Laputa all keep dogs to guard their houses. Here at Laputa's there are now three dogs: a large, half-German Shepherd dog called Samson which has attached itself to me; Chaka, a black-and-white terrier; and Juno, a brown terrier bitch. One day I noticed a tiny puppy walking up to the house from God knows where. Juno was then almost small enough to put in my pocket and I watched with interest as she wandered round, taking possession of the house. She has been with us ever since and is perhaps the best watchdog we have. We also have a black cat called Bagheera. No visitor, whatever their nationality, has so far failed to associate this name with Kipling's *Jungle Book*.

With my failing sight I need someone to look after me and a cousin of Namitu's, Lopego, has constituted himself my bodyguard and sleeps in my room. One night when Lopego was not there, I was woken by a crash. Five men had arrived, smashed open the outside door with a rock and a few seconds later were in my room, the door of which was always open. The key of Laputa's room, directly opposite mine, was always kept on the outside of his door and was only used to keep his two-year-old son, Sandy, out of the room in the daytime. As the men came in, they turned this key locking Laputa, his wife and baby son in their room. That night only the Bushbaby and Talone were sleeping in the central room. I turned over and saw three hooded figures in the doorway by the light of a torch which they had briefly switched on. For a second or two I assumed it was part of a bad dream, but then, realizing what they were, I hoped they weren't going to use pangas. Instead they carried thick, heavy sticks and two of them rained blows on me, luckily missing my head. In the dark, I sensed one of them beside me, rolled over, shouted, 'Get out of here, damn you!', kicked hard with my heel and started to get out of bed. I evidently got the man where it hurts most. He dropped his stick and next moment they were all gone. It was strange that our dogs had not barked or attacked these men. It has been suggested that they gave them meat to keep them quiet, or that one or more of them was well-known to the dogs. It was curious that while they were beating me, I could sense the blows but felt no pain. Two days later my left arm and both legs above the knee had turned completely black. The whole thing was an interesting experience but one which I have no desire to repeat.

This was the first of such attacks here in Maralal and in every case the men have beaten up the owner before robbing his house or shop. This is what happened when nine such thugs broke into Laputa's younger brother Rupalen's shop and stole everything in it including the money, after severely beating up Rupalen. As yet the police have failed to catch any of them. When they interviewed me the police said they were sorry I had not killed one of my attackers so that they would know who they were. Lopego never ceases to regret that he was away and was unable to kill at least one. Had he been there I am sure that he would have succeeded, using his iron-shod club.

Lopego is a tall, rather thin boy of seventeen, now in the eighth grade of his school at Maralal, where he has been a prefect for the past two years. He is happy, always keen to help and, unlike the others, undemanding. He enjoys working and has always been at the top, or close to the top, of his class. Both Lopego and Rupalen are enthusiastic Scouts. Rupalen has recently been appointed the District Area Commissioner of Scouts and Lopego is his deputy.

Over the years, my nephews Tom Reeves and James Harvey and a number of my close friends including Adrian House, Sebastian Verney, Paul McDermott, Frank Steele, Alexander Luce and Alexander Maitland, among others, have come and stayed with us here for varying lengths of time – from my point of view, the longer the better. They have been warned that living conditions are pretty basic, that the best we can do for them is a mattress on the floor of the verandah-room, and the food is always the same for them as for the rest of us. We always eat dinner in the kitchen, nine or ten of us together, in a comparatively small space. The five- and six-year-olds, even Sandy, Laputa's two-year-old son, perch wherever they can sit, to eat the food which one or other of us will have been cooking. The food does not vary, though it tastes different depending on who has cooked it, perhaps Namitu, or Lopego or even the Bushboy. They cook a large bowl of white maize-meal cake called *ugali* and chapattis which are eaten with a goat stew containing grated potatoes and carrots, chopped cabbage, onions and tomatoes, flavoured with chillies and a mixed spice called Roiko, all floating in a thick and generally delicious soup. People have said to me, 'We can't understand how you can eat the same food for dinner day in and day out'; I answer, 'But, after all, the Scots eat porridge every morning for breakfast,' though admittedly we don't have the pipes to help it down. I do run to porridge or cornflakes, sometimes an egg for my breakfast, which I eat in the sitting room, and Kibiriti most often gives me lunch in his house which is usually an excellent and very filling chopped liver in a thick soup with a bowl of rice. Or the ever-hospitable Siddiq Bhola gives me a more varied Pakistani meal in his house in Maralal. In our house, tea is the staple drink, or water, though I sometimes have coffee for breakfast, which I eat by myself or with any friends who are living with me. For breakfast the others eat bread which is included in the rations we buy each day in the town.

Some visitors enjoy being taken by the children to spend a night in their dark, smoke-filled *manyattas* nearby and thus see Samburu life at close quarters. Before they go there I tell them to buy a goat for the evening meal their hosts provide. When the goat is killed, children usually take it in turns to drink the blood as it gushes from its throat. One or two young tourists have done the same, something I myself could never have done.

This basic way of life may well have been a shock to some of my visitors, but having adapted themselves to it, they one and all appear to have enjoyed it. It has given them a close association with Africans, especially the children, which as normal visitors to this country they could never have experienced. I know that Frank Steele, Alex Maitland and my nephew, Tom Reeves, have enjoyed their visits here enormously and the mere mention of their names arouses enthusiasm among my families.

CHAPTER ELEVEN

Kenya, My Sanctuary

THE SAMBURU HAVE ALWAYS been cattle-owning pastoralists, but their ever-increasing numbers and the fact that a man's status depends on the number of his cows, whose possession means more to him than money, leads today to appalling overgrazing and consequent ruination of the land. In colonial times, British officials were constantly striving to prevent this, but there was no consistency of policy. Unlike the Sudan where, for instance, Guy Moore served as a DC in Kutum for as long as sixteen years, the DCs in Kenya were usually transferred every two years when they went on leave. Constant interference by different DCs with their cattle caused understandable resentment among the Samburu. Today there is no attempt to enforce any grazing policy, and large areas, even after heavy rains, have immediately been grazed bare.

Both the white settlers and the Samburu claimed possession of the Lorogi plateau, regarded by the settlers as one of the most fertile grazing areas in the Highlands. It was eventually awarded to the Samburu. Now much of it is as bare as a billiard table; every time the grass appears after rain, it is torn up by many hundreds of sheep, goats and cattle and is gone within a few days. Under such circumstances, sheep and cattle, since they can only graze, are more destructive than goats or camels. For this reason I feel certain that camels will eventually replace cows among the Samburu.

In 1979, 75 per cent of the Samburu cattle died as a result

of the drought. Everywhere, as I motored about I came across one carcass and then another, marking a route by which they had been moved in a desperate attempt to save them. Though it was tragic to see this happen, I felt at the time that the diminution of their herds might save the land. However, ten years later, their cattle were even more numerous and consequently the problem of over-grazing had reasserted itself.

In 1992–93 there has been another appalling drought in all the low country between Marsabit, Wamba and Baragoi, and even camels have died. At Maralal we have had some occasional heavy storms, but coming in December and January, out of season, they have been sporadic and very local. In April 1993 we were still waiting for the rains. So often I watched with hope the rainclouds gathering in the evening, only to see them disperse with despair.

I have copies of all my father's dispatches to the Foreign Office from 1910–18. There is no mention in them of any serious drought in the country during that period. Since then I am aware of no such drought in Ethiopia until the 1973 drought in Wollo whose consequences contributed to the ultimate overthrow of Haile Selassie. This was the first of a succession of catastrophic droughts that have occurred in the country. In the Sudan during the Mahdiya in 1889, a drought did occur and was followed by widespread famine, made worse by the conscription into the Dervish army of cultivators; and this decimated the population. I know of no other such occurrence in the Sudan until recent years.

Similarly in Kenya, serious droughts, especially in the north, appear to be a recent phenomenon. All this would seem to confirm the occurrence of a climatic change in the world attributable, I have always felt, to a culmination of pollution discharged into the air by cars, aeroplanes, factories and the like.

Since I have been living in Kenya, I have seen a rising material prosperity throughout the country, and one indication of this is the enormous increase in the number of privately owned cars. Thirty years ago when I first came to Nairobi, there were comparatively few cars in the streets. Now at certain hours the congestion is such that it is quicker to walk anywhere than travel in a car. Such a situation is now worldwide and can only grow worse. A hundred years ago there were no cars and no aeroplanes. Now we can look forward to a future when most Chinese families will own a car.

In 1960, the Samburu at Maralal still wore their traditional dress; but since Independence an increasing number of men and women have taken to wearing European clothes, especially in Maralal itself. Until after the 1990 initiation ceremonies almost all the previous warriors still dressed as *moran*. Now the recent initiates are mostly at school, wearing school uniform. Many of the old men, however, still wear the customary red blanket, but more and more women and girls have abandoned their blue robes for European fashions.

Universal education is having a profound effect on the lives of the Samburu. In Kenya, fathers are supposed to send all their children to school otherwise they could be fined. All boys should spend eight years in a primary school and all those who make the grade – if their parents can afford it – spend a further four years in a secondary school and four years in a university. Inevitably, any boy who has spent even four years in a primary school will no longer be content to go on living in his *manyatta* and herd his animals as he would have done in the past. Many of them now drift into Maralal where they are known as the 'Plastic Boys' and hang about the streets with the ultimate object of getting to Nairobi and finding a job. But a large number even of Kenya's university graduates today cannot find employment. In colonial times, when admittedly the population was much smaller, there was virtually no unemployment, nor were there any real slums in Nairobi.

Today, the population in Kenya continues to increase at an alarming rate every year. This is made worse in a country with a large Roman Catholic following by the papal ban on artificial methods of birth control. This ban, with its consequent prohibition on the use of condoms, must also have a serious effect on the spread of AIDS. The disintegration of traditional life due to universal education, combined with the population explosion, has resulted in increased unemployment and the growth of slum conditions in Kenya's towns and cities. And yet ironically the newspapers recently reported that farmers were finding it difficult to recruit labour. Despite these problems, implicit in universal education, I would not wish to deprive any enterprising boy of the opportunities which it affords. But I question the value of compelling all boys to go to school, when it offers no future advantage to so many of them.

Except for Laputa's two-year-old son and baby daughter, all the children in our house varying in age from nine to seventeen are at school where, with the exceptions of geography and world history, they acquire an impressive general education. They are taught only African geography which is confined to Kenya, Tanzania and Uganda. I was amazed to find that none of them had any idea where the Nile went when it left Uganda, or where America and China were to be found on a map of the world which I had pinned on the wall. After only two evenings' explanation even the youngest was able to point out where India, Iraq and Germany, for instance, were situated. In the course of an evening I may be asked questions about recent world history, which is not taught in school; for example, who fought against whom in the last war. I consider the natural intelligence and curiosity of these boys certainly the equal of any random group of English schoolboys. I always speak to them in English so that they should acquire a proper grasp of the language. English is still the official language of the country and is widely spoken. This has had a disastrous effect on my Swahili.

Two years ago, while we were sitting in the kitchen, one of the older boys came into the room and said, 'What does delicious mean?' The Bushbaby, a naturally silent little boy, then aged six or seven, who spoke Swahili and Samburu but apparently no word of English answered, 'Delicious food.' We were utterly astounded. Otherwise he refused to speak any English, but would stand up, shut the door, hold up a hand, shut his eyes or fan the charcoal stove when told to do so in English. A fortnight later, he unexpectedly started to talk in English to me. Now, two years later, he invariably gets full marks for his English exams at school.

Much of Kenya today is overrun by tourists. Fortunately as yet we get comparatively few in Maralal. Inevitably I am known to some of them from my books and if they see me in the town they usually come up to me. Sometimes I ask one, or perhaps two, of them to come and spend the night; by so doing I have met some interesting people and later often get letters from them. The 'Turkana buses' – actually lorries in which tourists sit back-to-back facing outwards – stop in Maralal on the way to Loiengalani on Lake Turkana. Then some thirty tourists, each with one or two cameras, jump down and advance on individuals in the crowd to take photographs. They make a pretence of objecting to being photographed whereupon the tour operator offers them money which of course they have been expecting. I hate this and I feel it is degrading. I have never paid anybody to take his photograph and never intend to. The photographs I have taken have been of people among whom I lived or with whom I was travelling, or others who knew and accepted me and my companions. In 1983, when I went to the Pushkar Fair in Rajasthan, I longed to take close-up portraits of some of these striking-looking Pathans but to do so would have been an intrusion; so I contented myself with some rather pointless general photographs. I have often been asked by someone looking at a photograph in my book *Visions of a Nomad*, 'How many photographs did you take to get that one?' Almost invariably the answer is, 'Just that one.'

Photographers have sometimes telephoned me in my London flat and said, 'Can we come and take a photograph of you?' They then go on clicking away until they have exposed a couple of rolls of film. I could never bring myself to take photographs like this, let alone use an automatic camera. I select a subject with care and take one photograph, possibly two. When travelling in Arabia and the Marshes, and indeed in Kenya, I would take with me perhaps twelve rolls of film to last me nine months. On my journey in Tanzania with John Newbould in 1963, I was anxious to photograph some Maasai we encountered, but they genuinely refused to be photographed. I therefore walked about, pointing my camera at nothing in an absorbed manner; after a while one of them asked if he could look through it. He did so and soon they were all looking at each other enthusiastically through the camera. After that there could be no further opposition to me doing the same. This was when I got some of my best results.

In Arabia and in the Marshes I used a Leica II with its 50mm standard lens and a hand-held light meter, but when I came to Kenya I had exchanged the Leica II for a Leicaflex and added a 35mm wide-angle lens, a 90mm portrait lens which I hardly ever used, and a 135mm telephoto lens. In fact, however, almost all my photographs have been taken with the 50mm standard lens. I keep a yellow filter permanently on my camera and I have never had a flash or a tripod. I know absolutely nothing about the mechanics of a camera, nor could I possibly develop the films which I have taken. I took them originally to James Sinclair in Whitehall to be developed, where K.B. Fleming took over the developing and printing of the films. When Sinclair's packed up, Mr Fleming continued to do this for me, saying he did it in the kitchen sink when his wife was not using it. Regrettably, he died recently. Today I rely with every confidence on Ron Clark.

Many people have expressed surprise that I did not take up animal photography. This could never have given me an equivalent tension and excitement to hunting. Although, of course, I have taken photographs of animals in Kenya, innumerable photographs have already been taken of these animals by others, most of them from cars. My main interest in photography has been in portraits of people, whereas generally speaking to me one lion, elephant or buffalo looks very much like another, without the fascinating variety of a human face.

I have often photographed landscapes which, after all, are the setting for my portraits of the inhabitants. There are splendid wide-sweeping views from high on the slopes of Mount Kenya; and impressive views from the summit of Mount Nyiru, northwards over Lake Turkana and southwards down the Suguta. But no other view in the NFD, or anywhere else in Kenya, rivals the spectacle from Malossa. I remember one of my visitors saying as he looked on it, 'I have seen nothing to compare with this in the Drakensbergs'. Malossa is perhaps an hour's drive from Maralal. Here the grassy escarpment ends abruptly in a very precipitous slope covered in places with vegetation, falling almost sheer to the Rift Valley 4000 feet or more below. From the crescent-shaped escarpment known as 'the Viewpoint', the scene is interestingly varied. Nearby, to the west, an unexpected, half-hidden gorge severs the escarpment and, on the far side of this, the escarpment rises to a bare pinnacle. To the north-east, a series of bluffs offers a different picture, according to where one stands or sits. This is a dramatic setting for the view beyond, made all the more effective by its very concentration.

From the foot of the escarpment, scattered acacias, looking minute, and bare tawny spaces scarred by black tracks of fires, extend to a series of alternating rises and depressions, among which somewhere lies the Suguta valley; then, just visible in the distance, are faint mountains on the Ugandan border.

I came here one morning when the entire valley beneath me was hidden by white cloud. I found myself standing in sunshine above a platform of cloud reaching up almost to my feet, so close that I could touch it with my stick. This was a curiously unreal experience. Nowhere was the horizon visible, but through occasional gaps in the cloud I could get glimpses of the valley floor which seemed unbelievably far away.

As in Arabia and in the Iraqi Marshes, my life here in Maralal, as I have described, has always been concerned with individuals rather than the community as a whole. But, for me, these individuals have to be part of their traditional setting. In each case it has been my desire to be as closely associated with them as possible. Sandy Field once observed, 'If you want to live in Kenya why on earth don't you build yourself a proper house, live comfortably and have proper servants?' Sandy has never understood that I don't want either. During the five most contented years of my life when I lived with the Rashid in southern Arabia, everything I owned went into my saddle bags. My camera was the only object that I brought with me which they did not possess. I certainly believe the more possessions you own the more they rob you of your freedom. I inherited a very attractive flat in Chelsea from my mother; as well as being very well furnished, it had some fine and valuable pictures and drawings and a remarkable collection of books. I have spent three months a year in this flat, but I have never had any desire to live there permanently. The flat itself and its contents have, in reality, meant comparatively little to me, and even less now that my mother and our housekeeper, Mollie Emtage, are dead. Laputa's house in which I now live in Maralal gives me shelter from the weather and has been an assembly point for the Africans with whom I live.

I moved to Laputa's house when Lawi became increasingly involved in politics. Lawi eventually constructed a spacious three-roomed concrete house adjoining the house which we had built together. Unexpectedly, the two harmonize, one with the other. Here he lives comfortably with his wife and Tyson, their lively three-year-old son. As the mayor, he was very busy and his house was often occupied with visitors who had come to see him on official business. Lawi unfortunately insisted on resigning from the urban council in order to stand for Maralal as a Kanu candidate in the recent elections. He was opposed by another Kanu candidate who won the seat, a brother of General Lenges, the army commander. Lawi was later employed as co-ordinator in a film being made by Americans in South Africa, involving more than a hundred Samburu. Lawi flew with them to Johannesburg, near which the film was being made. At short notice he had to obtain passports for them and all the other necessary documents, which he did very competently. The film centres on a young Samburu who becomes an international basketball player. Recently I have seen rather less of Lawi since he became involved in this film.

Looking back over my life I have never wanted a master and servant relationship with my retainers. Even in the Sudan as an Assistant DC when I travelled with camels, I instinctively and invariably slept and sat on the ground and shared my food with those who were travelling with me. This, of course, is what I did in Arabia and in the Marshes of Iraq and I have continued to do so in Kenya.

In Arabia and in the Marshes I had a very close relationship with some of the people with whom I lived; this I cherished. While I was with the Rashid I would gladly have been assimilated by them; but I would never have wished that I had been born an Arab instead of an Englishman, for I am proud to be English and could wish to be nothing else. Similarly, family pride, rather than any form of religious conviction, would forbid me from becoming a Muslim. What I valued was their companionship. Here in Kenya the people among whom I am living are involved in my life and I am involved in theirs. I pay them no wages and have never regarded them as servants, but as part of my family. I have endeavoured to help them establish themselves and this has often involved me with considerable expense; it has, however, been my pleasure to do this. I own neither a house nor a car. Instead, having lived in Lawi's house, I now live in Laputa's and make use of the Land Rover which I bought for Kibiriti.

Happily, I have never been conscious of any colour prejudice and was pleased when Lawi once remarked, 'People here say that you regard your English and African friends alike.' I believe that in England it is far more difficult than it is here for anyone to be accepted as part of a family unless they really belong to it. Here, on the contrary, it is relatively easy because a father-and-son relationship is inherent in so many of their customs.

During my life I have never involved myself in politics nor indeed taken anything other than a superficial interest in them. Today with one or two exceptions I do not know the names of anybody in the British government and the same applies to the government in Kenya. The life I have led has seldom given me the opportunity to read a newspaper. There was a radio in my mother's flat, to which I seldom listened, and I have never owned nor wished to own a radio while I have been abroad. However, Lopego now owns a radio and with my failing sight and consequent inability to read I increasingly listen to it.

I have been appalled at what I hear. Never in the past has there been such almost universal chaos and bloodshed in Africa – in the Sudan, Somalia, Angola, Liberia, Mozambique and Zaire, for instance. In contrast to this, for thirty years ever since Independence, Kenya had had uninterrupted peace, stability and development, and was surely a model for other emergent African countries. The KANU government under Jomo Kenyatta had been dominated by the Kikuyu, but Moi in his mainly Kalenjin government included Kikuyu, Luo and other tribes, which seemed to me satisfactory. In Kenya, as in other African countries, tribalism, without doubt, has always been and still is the strongest political factor. Despite this, the Americans insisted on Moi agreeing to multi-party government and since then, over the past year, there have been more disturbances and more people killed than in the whole history of Kenya since Independence.

Ever since I left Oxford in 1933, I have never spent more than three, or occasionally four, months in England in any one year. I returned to London to be with my mother and to see my many friends, and acquaintances I have met abroad. For this reason, when I am in England now, I have no desire to be anywhere but in London; anyway, the English countryside means little to me. If I lived in the country I should really be confined to meeting my neighbours. Mollie Emtage had been with us for almost forty-five years. Until my mother died Mollie looked after her with devotion; and she looked after me with the same devotion until she died in 1991. Now to live alone in an empty flat, unable to read because of my failing sight, would be very desolate.

When I first came to Kenya, I intended to spend perhaps two years in the country travelling with camels in the Northern Frontier District, but since then I have come to regard Maralal as my home. It is here, among those whose lives I share today, that I hope to end my days.

Index